New York Academic Cont<

Standard 1 Social Studies: History of the United States and New York

Students will: use a variety of intellectual skills to demonstrate their understanding of major ideas, eras, themes, developments, and turning points in the history of the United States and New York.

1.1 The study of New York State and United States history requires an analysis of the development of American culture, its diversity and multicultural context, and the ways people are unified by many values, practices, and traditions.

1.2 Important ideas, social and cultural values, beliefs, and traditions from New York State and United States history illustrate the connections and interactions of people and events across time and from a variety of perspectives.

1.3 Study about the major social, political, economic, cultural, and religious developments in New York State and United States history involves learning about the important roles and contributions of individuals and groups.

1.4 The skills of historical analysis include the ability to: explain the significance of historical evidence; weigh the importance, reliability, and validity of evidence; understand the concept of multiple causation; understand the importance of changing and competing interpretations of different historical developments.

Standard 2 Social Studies: World History

Students will: use a variety of intellectual skills to demonstrate their understanding of major ideas, eras, themes, developments, and turning points in world history and examine the broad sweep of history from a variety of perspectives.

2.1 The study of world history requires an understanding of world cultures and civilizations, including an analysis of important ideas, social and cultural values, beliefs, and traditions. This study also examines the human condition and the connections and interactions of people across time and space and the ways different people view the same event or issue from a variety of perspectives.

2.2 Establishing timeframes, exploring different periodizations, examining themes across time and within cultures, and focusing on important turning points in world history help organize the study of world cultures and civilizations.

2.3 Study of the major social, political, cultural, and religious developments in world history involves learning about the important roles and contributions of individuals and groups.

2.4 The skills of historical analysis include the ability to investigate differing and competing interpretations of the theories of history, hypothesize about why interpretations change over time, explain the importance of historical evidence, and understand the concepts of change and continuity over time.

Standard 3 Social Studies: Geography

Students will: use a variety of intellectual skills to demonstrate their understanding of the geography of the interdependent world in which we live—local, national, and global—including the distribution of people, places, and environments over the Earth's surface.

3.1 Geography can be divided into six essential elements which can be used to analyze important historic, geographic, economic, and environmental questions and issues. These six elements include: the world in spatial terms, places and regions, physical settings (including natural resources), human systems, environment and society, and the use of geography. (Adapted from The National Geography Standards, 1994: Geography for Life)

3.2 Geography requires the development and application of the skills of asking and answering geographic questions; analyzing theories of geography; and acquiring, organizing, and analyzing geographic information. (Adapted from: The National Geography Standards, 1994: Geography for Life)

Standard 4 Social Studies: Economics

Students will: use a variety of intellectual skills to demonstrate their understanding of how the United States and other societies develop economic systems and associated institutions to allocate scarce resources, how major decision-making units function in the U.S. and other national economies, and how an economy solves the scarcity problem through market and nonmarket mechanisms.

4.1 The study of economics requires an understanding of major economic concepts and systems, the principles of economic decision making, and the interdependence of economies and economic systems throughout the world.

4.2 Economics requires the development and application of the skills needed to make informed and well-reasoned economic decisions in daily and national life.

Standard 5 Social Studies: Civics, Citizenship, and Government

Students will: use a variety of intellectual skills to demonstrate their understanding of the necessity for establishing governments; the governmental system of the U.S. and other nations; the U.S. Constitution; the basic civic values of American constitutional democracy; and the roles, rights, and responsibilities of citizenship, including avenues of participation.

5.1 The study of civics, citizenship, and government involves learning about political systems; the purposes of government and civic life; and the differing assumptions held by people across time and place regarding power, authority, governance, and law. (Adapted from The National Standards for Civics and Government, 1994)

5.2 The state and federal governments established by the Constitutions of the United States and the State of New York embody basic civic values (such as justice, honesty, self-discipline, due process, equality, majority rule with respect for minority rights, and respect for self, others, and property), principles, and practices and establish a system of shared and limited government. (Adapted from The National Standards for Civics and Government, 1994)

5.3 Central to civics and citizenship is an understanding of the roles of the citizen within American constitutional democracy and the scope of a citizen's rights and responsibilities.

5.4 The study of civics and citizenship requires the ability to probe ideas and assumptions, ask and answer analytical questions, take a skeptical attitude toward questionable arguments, evaluate evidence, formulate rational conclusions, and develop and refine participatory skills.

The World

PROGRAM AUTHORS

James A. Banks
Kevin P. Colleary
Linda Greenow
Walter C. Parker
Emily M. Schell
Dinah Zike

CONTRIBUTORS

Raymond C. Jones
Irma M. Olmedo

 Macmillan/McGraw-Hill

Volume I

PROGRAM AUTHORS

James A. Banks, Ph.D.
Kerry and Linda Killinger Professor of
Diversity Studies and Director
Center for Multicultural Education
University of Washington
Seattle, Washington

Kevin Colleary, Ed.D.
Curriculum and Teaching Department
Graduate School of Education
Fordham University
New York, New York

Linda Greenow, Ph.D.
Associate Professor and Chair
Department of Geography
State University of New York at
New Paltz
New Paltz, New York

Walter C. Parker, Ph.D.
Professor of Social Studies Education,
Adjunct Professor of Political Science
University of Washington
Seattle, Washington

Emily M. Schell, Ed.D.
Visiting Professor, Teacher Education
San Diego State University
San Diego, California

Dinah Zike
Educational Consultant
Dinah-Mite Activities, Inc.
San Antonio, Texas

CONTRIBUTORS

Raymond C. Jones, Ph.D.
Director of Secondary Social Studies
Education
Wake Forest University
Wake Forest, North Carolina

Irma M. Olmedo
Associate Professor
University of Illinois-Chicago
College of Education
Chicago, Illinois

HISTORIANS/SCHOLARS

Rabbi Pamela Barmash, Ph.D.
Associate Professor of Hebrew Bible
and Biblical Hebrew and Director
Program in Jewish, Islamic and Near
Eastern Studies
Washington University
St. Louis, Missouri

Thomas Bender, Ph.D.
Professor of History
New York University
New York, New York

Ned Blackhawk
Associate Professor of History and
American Indian Studies
University of Wisconsin
Madison, Wisconsin

Chun-shu Chang
Department of History
University of Michigan
Ann Arbor, Michigan

Manuel Chavez, Ph.D.
Associate Director, Center for Latin
American & Caribbean Studies,
Assistant Professor, School of
Journalism
Michigan State University
East Lansing, Michigan

Sheilah F. Clarke-Ekong, Ph.D.
Professor of Anthropology
University of Missouri
St. Louis, Missouri

Lawrence Dale, Ph.D.
Director, Center for Economic
Education
Arkansas State University
Jonesboro, Arkansas

Mac Dixon-Fyle, Ph.D.
Professor of History
DePauw University.
Greencastle, Indiana

Carl W. Ernst
William R. Kenan, Jr., Distinguished
Professor
Department of Religious Studies
Director, Carolina Center for the
Study of the Middle East and Muslim
Civilizations
University of North Carolina
Chapel Hill, North Carolina

Brooks Green, Ph.D.
Associate Professor of Geography
University of Central Arkansas
Conway, Arkansas

Students with print disabilities may be eligible to obtain an accessible, audio version of the pupil edition of this textbook. Please call Recording for the Blind & Dyslexic at 1-800-221-4792 for complete information.

The McGraw-Hill Companies

Macmillan
McGraw-Hill

Copyright © 2009 by The McGraw-Hill Companies, Inc. All rights reserved. Except as permitted under the United States Copyright Act, no part of this publication may be reproduced or distributed in any form or by any means, or stored in a database or retrieval system, without prior permission of the publisher.

Send all inquires to:
Macmillan/McGraw-Hill
8787 Orion Place
Columbus, OH 43240-4027

MHID: 0-02-152301-0
ISBN: 978-0-02-152301-6
Printed in the United States of America.
2 3 4 5 6 7 8 9 10   079/043   13 12 11 10 09

The World

CONTENTS, Volume 1

Unit 1 Rivers and Civilizations 17

How does geography affect civilizations?

Reference Section

Skills and Features

Maps

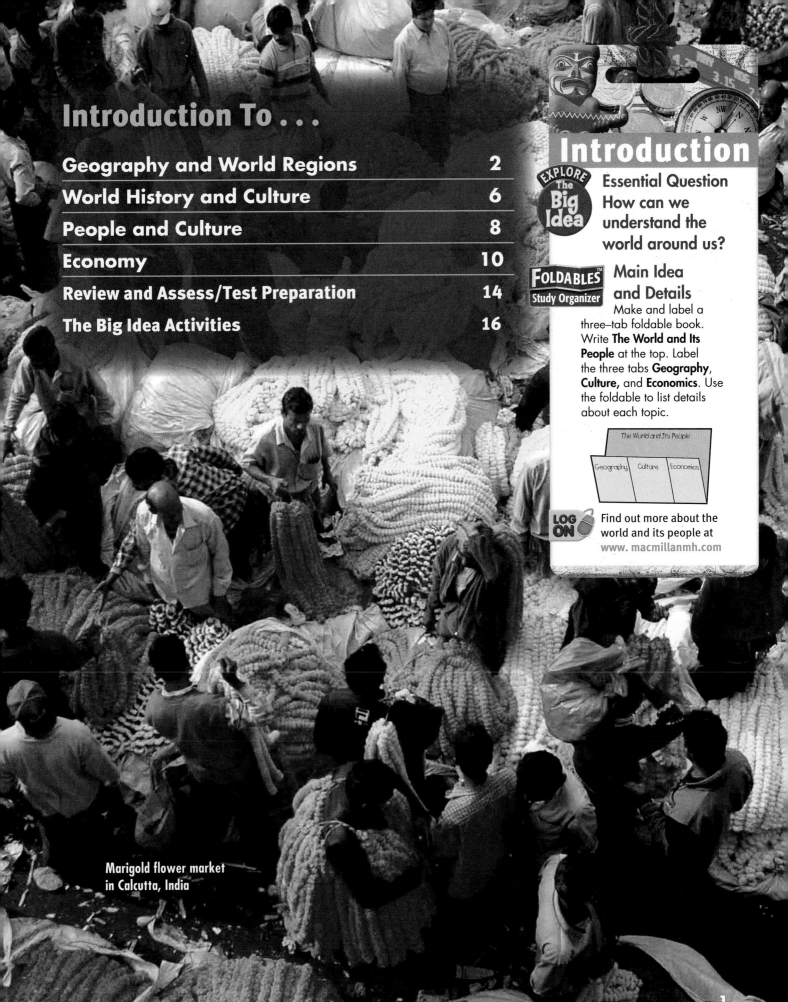

Introduction To . . .

Introduction

EXPLORE The Big Idea

Essential Question
How can we understand the world around us?

FOLDABLES Study Organizer

Main Idea and Details
Make and label a three–tab foldable book. Write **The World and Its People** at the top. Label the three tabs **Geography, Culture,** and **Economics.** Use the foldable to list details about each topic.

The World and Its People

Geography | Culture | Economics

LOG ON Find out more about the world and its people at www. macmillanmh.com

Marigold flower market in Calcutta, India

1

Geography and World Regions

VOCABULARY

geography p. 2

physical regions p. 2

climate p. 2

New York Academic Content Standards
3.1, 3.2

Geography is the study of Earth's surface—its land, water, and its weather. Geography also includes the study of people in their environment. It traces the movement of people over time. Geography can give you insight into the rise and fall of civilizations.

Ⓐ KEY IDEAS

Social studies is an exciting and challenging subject. And geography plays a major role in understanding the world and its people. In the following pages, you will be introduced to some key ideas about geography. These ideas will come up again and again as you read this book.

The Continents

Earth can be divided into **physical regions**. A physical region is a natural environment with features such as coastlines, mountains, and rivers. Earth also has a wide variety of **climates**. A climate is the weather of a region over a long period of time. Continents are large physical regions with their own features. Earth's continents are described on the following pages.

As you will see, many people live on each continent. People can change their environment to meet their needs. They build canals to connect rivers and roads to connect cities. They cut down forests, plant crops, and build dams. They control the flow of water for transportation and energy.

The snow-covered peak of Mount Kilimanjaro ▶

QUICK CHECK

Summarize **Name some features that define a physical region.**

Africa

Africa makes up about 20 percent of the Earth's land and contains about 12.5 percent of the world's population. Central Africa lies along the Equator. The Sahara, the world's largest desert, covers much of northern Africa.

POPULATION: 915 million

AREA: 11.7 million square miles

HIGHEST ELEVATION: Mount Kilimanjaro (Tanzania) 19,341 feet

LONGEST RIVER: Nile River (Egypt) 4,160 miles

Africa

Victoria Falls on the Zambezi River in Zimbabwe, Africa

Asia

Asia is the largest continent. It makes up 30 percent of Earth's land and holds 60 percent of Earth's people! Asia stretches from the Arctic to the Equator and has many climate zones. It also contains the Himalaya, the world's tallest mountain range.

Asia

Rice paddies at the foot of the Guilin Mountains in China

POPULATION: 3.6 billion

AREA: 19.2 million square miles

HIGHEST ELEVATION: Mount Everest (Nepal) 29,028 feet

LONGEST RIVER: Chang Jiang (China) 3,434 miles

Australia and Oceania

Australia and Oceania are located southeast of Asia. Australia has the smallest landmass of all the continents. Oceania is made up of thousands of islands, some no larger than a soccer field. Others are as large as the state of Colorado.

Australia and Oceania

POPULATION: 34 million

AREA: 3.3 million square miles

HIGHEST ELEVATION: Mount Kosciusko (Australia) 7,310 feet

LONGEST RIVER: Murray River (Australia) 1,609 miles

Uluru, also called Ayers Rock, Australia

Europe

Europe

Europe makes up about 7 percent of Earth's land. Europe and Asia are actually parts of the same landmass called Eurasia. The Urals, a mountain range in Russia, divides Europe from Asia.

POPULATION: 807 million

AREA: 8.9 million square miles

HIGHEST ELEVATION: Mount Elbrus (Russia) 18,510 feet

LONGEST RIVER: Volga River (Russia) 2,293 miles

A fjord in Scandinavia

North America

North America includes Canada, the United States, Mexico, all the countries of Central America, and the islands of the Caribbean. It makes up nearly 17 percent of Earth's land and contains about 13 percent of the population.

The Colorado River at the base of the Grand Canyon

North America

POPULATION: 512 million

AREA: 9.4 million square miles

HIGHEST ELEVATION: Mount McKinley (Alaska) 20,320 feet

LONGEST RIVER: Mississippi-Missouri (United States) 3,877 miles

South America

South America is connected to North America by a strip of land on the border of Colombia. The Equator crosses the northern part of South America. This continent makes up 12 percent of Earth's land and contains 5 percent of the world's population.

South America

POPULATION: 371 million

AREA: 6.9 million square miles

HIGHEST ELEVATION: Mount Aconcagua (Argentina) 22,834 feet

LONGEST RIVER: Amazon (Peru, Brazil) 3,915 miles

The Great Barrier Reef off the coast of Australia

Angel Falls in Venezuela

World History and Culture

VOCABULARY

cultural region p. 6

archaeologist p. 7

anthropologist p. 7

ancestors p. 7

oral history p. 7

New York Academic Content Standards
2.1

Every time that you eat a meal, talk to your friends, or listen to music, you are participating in your culture. Culture is the whole way of life of any group or people. Culture includes traditions, customs, language, art, music, food, work, and beliefs.

B PEOPLE AND CULTURE

People create culture. They may compose a new song or come up with a new recipe. All people are influenced by their culture. Culture helps to define a group of people.

You have read that geographers identify places on Earth as physical regions. They also understand the world by defining **cultural regions.** A cultural region is an area influenced by a certain culture.

One physical region can contain many cultural regions. A culture can be unique, or it can share things with other cultures. As you read, you will learn that culture can affect people as much as geography can.

Archaeologists working in China

Learning About the Past

What happens when there is no record or written history left by a culture? Well, that is where **archaeologists** come in! Archaeologists are scientists who study the remains of human culture to learn about life long ago. They study things that are very old. They look at human remains, such as bones and hair. They also study the things that early humans made, such as tools, pottery, cloth, and jewelry.

Other scientists also help us to understand the past. **Anthropologists** study human cultures, patterns of migration, settlements, and human ancestors. **Ancestors** are family members who lived a long time ago.

A West African storyteller reciting oral histories

Anthropologists often listen to **oral histories**, stories told aloud and passed from one generation to the next. You can listen to your own family's oral history—just ask your relatives. They can tell you stories about your family's traditions, or how your family came to live where you are today.

QUICK CHECK

Make Inferences **Why might a physical region have many cultural regions?**

Golden barges at a festival in Thailand ▶

People and Culture

People in a culture not only share a language and traditions, they share values, too. Values are beliefs about what they consider to be important in life.

New York Academic Content Standards

2.1

C CULTURAL VALUES

Values include ideas about what is right or wrong, helpful or harmful, what is a success, and what is a failure. One culture may value independence, freedom, and earning money. Another culture may value cooperation and respect for the family. Consider your own culture. What are its values?

A culture can express its values through religious beliefs. A culture may contain a single religion or the beliefs of many religions.

Governments reflect values too. Officials and leaders that make up a government help to maintain the values of a culture. They may protect rights, collect taxes, or enforce laws.

A Muslim family at a religious feast

A bullet train in Japan ▼

How Culture Changes

Cultures are very complex, and they are changing all the time. They can change because of **innovation**. An innovation is a new idea or way of doing something. Cultures can also change through interaction with other cultures.

One kind of interaction is cultural **diffusion**. Diffusion occurs when part of a culture spreads through many other cultures or areas. For example, many people across North and South America speak Spanish because these continents were conquered and settled by people from Spain.

Another kind of interaction is cultural **infusion**. Infusion is the introduction of one thing into another. Spanish explorers returned to Spain from the Americas with chocolate. Drinking hot chocolate is now part of Spanish culture.

Three generations at the dining table

A voter casting a ballot in Central Asia

QUICK CHECK

Making Inferences **In what ways would the television programs of one culture influence another?**

An economy is the way that goods and services are produced and distributed. It helps to define a country.

D BUYING AND SELLING

Producers are people who provide services and make goods people buy. **Consumers** are people who buy goods or use services. The economy of a country includes the activities of all consumers and producers within that country.

Suppose you want to buy a CD and a book. You want both equally, but you only have enough money to buy one or the other. If the book costs less, however, then it would be the better choice because you would get more enjoyment per dollar spent. This is called a cost-benefit decision. If you buy the book, then the CD is your opportunity cost. Opportunity cost is the value of the thing that you did not buy. Businesses make cost-benefit decisions much like this every day.

VOCABULARY

producers p. 10

consumers p. 10

gross domestic product p. 11

manufacturing economy p. 12

service economy p. 13

New York Academic Content Standards

4.1, 4.2

A fruit stand in Germany

Economic Systems

Some countries have a free-enterprise system. People can own and run their own businesses. People who start their own businesses are called entrepreneurs.

Entrepreneurs want to make a profit. Profit is the money that a business makes after it pays the costs of running the business. Some businesses use investments from other people. An investment is money that is put into a business to help it succeed. A successful business returns some of the profit to the people who made the investments.

A few countries have command economies. Their governments decide what will be produced and what the products will cost.

GDP

Add up the cost of all goods and services in any country, and you have that country's

Gold items for sale in Hong Kong ▲

gross domestic product (GDP). In the United States, the GDP is in the trillions of dollars!

QUICK CHECK

Draw Conclusions What is the opportunity cost if you decide to buy a new shirt instead of a video game?

A colorful market in France ▼

MARKETPLACES

The marketplace describes any economy in action. It may refer to a small neighborhood shop or a worldwide industry.

Supply and Demand

Supply is the amount of any product or service available at any time. If the supply is large, prices will be low. If supply is scarce, prices will be high. Demand is how much of a product or service people want to buy. If demand is low, prices tend to be low. If demand is high, prices will be high, too.

Local Economy

A nation's economy is made up of many smaller, local economies. Local economies include the jobs and resources in a particular area. A rural economy might be based on farming. A port town may depend on fishing or tourism.

Some economies are **manufacturing economies**. A manufacturing economy is based on making products, such as cars, cell phones, paper, or steel.

Farm to Market

Harvested chilies are loaded onto trucks.

Farm workers harvest chilies.

Some chilies are transported to a local market.

Other areas may have a **service economy**. A service economy is based on providing services or doing certain tasks, such as computer programming or working in a hotel or a bank.

Most local economies are a mixture of manufacturing and service economies. How would you describe the economy of your area?

Global Economy

Almost all countries need products and services from other countries. This means that national economies around the world are interdependent. When one country sends its products to another country, those products are called exports. Exports are shipped from one country to another. When a country buys products and brings them across its borders, those products are called imports.

The economies of most nations expand by trading with other nations. Today many companies operate in more than one country, as part of the global economy.

QUICK CHECK

Make Inferences Why would one country import products from another country?

Some chilies go to a factory where they are made into sauce and bottled.

Bottled sauces are shipped around the world.

Chili sauce includes chili peppers, onions, garlic, and spices.

Consumers buy their favorite bottled sauce.

PICANTE SAUCE $2.99

13

Vocabulary

Write the word from the list below that matches each definition below.

climate   anthropologist

innovation   diffusion

archaeologist   producer

culture   geography

1. a new way of doing things
2. the spreading of one thing into another
3. a scientist who studies human culture
4. a region's weather over a long period of time
5. the study of Earth's surface
6. a person who makes goods or provides services
7. a scientist who studies the remains of human culture
8. the elements that make up the way of life of a people

Comprehension and Critical Thinking

9. **Geography** How can people change their environment?
10. **Critical Thinking** How does climate affect the way people live?
11. **Economics** What is the role of an entrepreneur in a free–enterprise system?
12. **Critical Thinking** Why would someone make an investment in a business?
13. **Economics** If there is little demand for a product, what will happen to its price?
14. **Critical Thinking** Why might the price of a product, like a wool coat or a gallon of gasoline, change over time?
15. **Culture** Why do anthropologists study oral histories?
16. **Critical Thinking** What can we learn about a culture by studying its tools and other remains?

New York English Language Arts Test Preparation

Directions
**Read this passage about celebrating the Lunar New Year.
Then answer questions 1 and 2.**

The Lunar New Year is the most important traditional Asian holiday. A lunar calendar begins a new year based on the moon, rather than the sun. For many Asians, the Lunar New Year Festival takes place during the second new moon of winter.

Asians around the world plan a feast for the festival. Many travel long distances to visit relatives. The largest migration of people each year is for the Lunar New Year.

Dancers dressed as lions and dragons parade through the streets. Their drums and gongs are believed to frighten away evil spirits and bring good fortune in the new year.

---

1 What is the main idea of this passage?

A Celebrations are very expensive.

B The Lunar New Year is an
important and symbolic celebration.

C Family traditions are only for holidays.

D The Lunar New Year is a good time for a vacation.

2 Which is a synonym for the word fortune in the sentence below?
"Their drums and gongs are believed to frighten away evil spirits and bring good fortune in the new year."

A disaster

B excitement

C fear

D luck

The Big Idea Activities

How can we understand the world around us?

Write About the Big Idea

Narrative Essay
Review your completed foldable. Think about the reasons we study other cultures. Use your foldable to organize your ideas before you write an essay to answer the Big Idea question, "How can we understand the world around us?" Be sure to begin with an introduction. Include one paragraph for each main idea. End with a concluding paragraph.

FOLDABLES™
Study Organizer

The World and Its People

Geography | Culture | Economics

Be an Anthropologist

Ask a parent, grandparent, aunt, uncle, or other relative or friend of the family to talk about their past.

Use a recorder or pencil and paper to take notes.

1. Before your meeting, think about what you would like to ask. Write your questions on a sheet of paper.

2. Meet with the person. Ask your relative or friend questions about childhood memories, education, prices, entertainment, and people who were important to him or her. Write or record each answer.

3. Share what you have learned with your classmates. If you recorded the person, you may want to play some of the recording for your class.

Compare oral histories with your classmates. What do they tell you about the culture the person lived in? How do they compare to your life today?

Rivers and Civilizations

Unit 1

 EXPLORE The Big Idea

Essential Question
How does geography affect civilizations?

 FOLDABLES Study Organizer

Cause and Effect
Make a layered book foldable to take notes as you read Unit 1. Your notes will help you answer the Big Idea question. Your foldable's title will be **How Geography Affects Civilizations**. Your foldable will have 4 layers, labeled **Mesopotamia, Egypt, India,** and **China**.

 LOG ON For more about Unit 1 go to www.macmillanmh.com

The Li River in China

PEOPLE, PLACES, and EVENTS

Otzi

Italian Alps

3300 B.C. | Old Stone Age man "Otzi" is murdered.

Hatshepsut

Luxor, Egypt

1473 B.C. | Pharaoh Hatshepsut sends an expedition to Punt.

4000 BC   2000 BC   1500 BC

"Otzi," an Old Stone Age man, is murdered in the **Italian Alps.**

Today you can see Otzi's tools and clothes at a museum in Bolzano, Italy.

Hatshepsut was the first female pharaoh of Egypt.

Today you can visit Hatshepsut's spectacular temple near **Luxor, Egypt.**

LOG ON For more about People, Places, and Events, visit www.macmillanmh.com

Asoka

Pataliputra

273 B.C.
Asoka rules Maurya Empire in India.

Qin Shihuangdi

Shensi Province

209 B.C.
Qin Shihuangdi orders his tomb built.

1000 BC   **500 BC**   **AD 1**

Asoka ruled India during more than 40 years of peace.

Today you can visit Patna, India, which used to be **Pataliputra,** Asoka's capital city.

Qin Shihuangdi was China's first emperor. His tomb was guarded by more than 7,000 clay statues of soldiers.

Today you can see these clay soldiers in **Shensi Province** in China.

Lesson 1

VOCABULARY

hunter-gatherer p. 21

environment p. 21

Old Stone Age p. 21

technology p. 21

artifact p. 22

READING SKILL

Cause and Effect
Complete the chart as you read. Write details that show the advantages for early people of living in groups.

Cause	→	Effect
	→	
	→	
	→	

New York Academic Content Standards
2.2, 3.1, 3.2

EARLY PEOPLE

Old Stone Age drawings from a cave in France

Visual Preview

How did early people adapt to their environment?

A Early humans used fire and made tools.

B We learn about early people from their artifacts.

PEOPLE OF THE OLD STONE AGE

Cartoons often show short "cave people" with sloping foreheads who carried clubs and wore animal skins. Scientific discoveries, though, have changed our thinking about these early people.

Early humans were as tall as we are today. Skeletons of these people show that they stood up straight. They were often healthy and strong, too!

Early Life

Early people had hard lives. Their skeletons show that they suffered serious injuries. They also had to search for food all of the time. They were **hunter-gatherers** who hunted animals and gathered wild plants for food. Early people knew a lot about their **environment**, or their surroundings. They knew which plants were good foods and medicines and which were poisonous.

Human life changed when people learned how to make fire. Perhaps someone came across a fire caused by lightning. Or maybe someone noticed sparks when certain stones were struck together. Having fire meant people could cook their food. Fire also provided light. In cold climates, fires helped people stay warm.

Until about 10,000 years ago, people could only make things from stone and wood. So this period in history is called the **Old Stone Age**.

The Earliest Tools

When early humans used a rock or a stick, they were using tools. Later, people sharpened stones to make axes. They also made needles from sharpened animal bones. These tools are an example of early **technology**. Technology is any tool or invention used to complete a task.

QUICK CHECK

Cause and Effect What changes did fire make in the way humans lived?

Asian hunters cross the Bering Strait about 25,000 years ago. ▶

21

STUDYING THE EVIDENCE

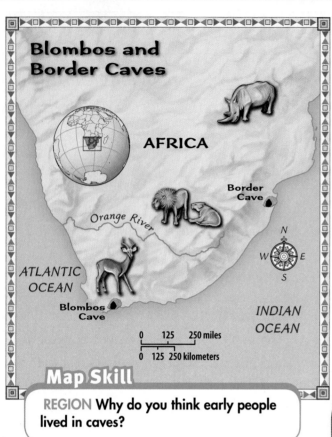

Blombos and Border Caves

AFRICA

Border Cave

Orange River

ATLANTIC OCEAN

Blombos Cave

0   125   250 miles

0   125   250 kilometers

INDIAN OCEAN

N W E S

Map Skill

REGION **Why do you think early people lived in caves?**

▲ Artifacts like the shell bead (left) and these arrowheads were found at Blombos Cave.

overlooked a warm grassland area with many animals. Old Stone Age people hunted these animals, including hippopotamuses and rhinoceroses.

QUICK CHECK

Cause and Effect **What did archaeologists learn from Border and Blombos Caves?**

Archaeologists, scientists who study early people, have learned about the Old Stone Age and other times by studying **artifacts.** Artifacts are objects made and used by people in the past. Bowls, needles, and other ordinary household items are common artifacts.

Two Caves

Some of the oldest human artifacts come from Africa. In 1940, a farmer discovered human bones at a site called Border Cave. The bones were about 40,000 years old! The cave also held thousands of Old Stone Age artifacts and bones of more than 40 kinds of animals.

Blombos Cave is also in South Africa. Archaeologists have found bone and stone tools here. Some of the artifacts are 70,000 years old. At that time, Blombos Cave

Check Understanding

1. **VOCABULARY** Write a summary of the Old Stone Age using these vocabulary words.

   hunter-gatherer   technology
   environment

2. **READING SKILL Cause and Effect** Use your chart from page 20 to write about why early people lived in groups.

Cause	→	Effect
	→	
	→	
	→	

3. **Write About It** How did location affect how early people lived?

Chart and Graph Skills

Read a Parallel Time Line

VOCABULARY

time line
parallel time line
century
decade
circa

A **time line** is a diagram of events arranged in order. A **parallel time line** shows two sets of dates on the same time line.

B.C. stands for "before Christ." A.D. (*anno Domini)* dates years from the birth of Jesus. Other time lines use C.E. for "common era" and B.C.E. for "before common era."

A **century** is 100 years. Ten years make a **decade**. You may also see **circa** or (c.) for "about" when the exact date is not known.

Life of Christopher Henshilwood

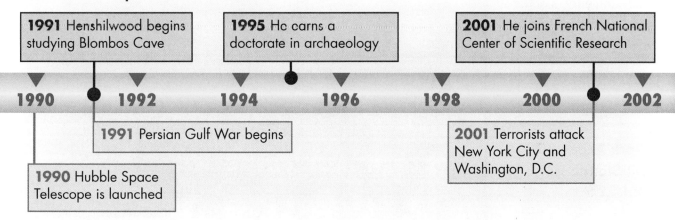

1991 Henshilwood begins studying Blombos Cave

1995 He earns a doctorate in archaeology

2001 He joins French National Center of Scientific Research

1990 · 1992 · 1994 · 1996 · 1998 · 2000 · 2002

1991 Persian Gulf War begins

1990 Hubble Space Telescope is launched

2001 Terrorists attack New York City and Washington, D.C.

Events in U.S. History

Learn It

Use the steps to read a parallel time line.

- Identify the time span. This time line covers the years from 1990 to 2002.

- Identify the periods on the time line. Each time period must be equal.

- Identify events on each time line.

- Compare the time lines. What events happened at or about the same time?

Try It

Use the time line to answer the questions:

- How many years after the Gulf War did Henshilwood earn his doctorate?

- Which two events happened in 2001?

Apply It

- Make a parallel time line of your life. Put events from your life on top. Put events in United States history on the bottom.

VOCABULARY

agriculture p. 25

surplus p. 25

specialize p. 25

barter p. 25

domesticate p. 26

READING SKILL

Cause and Effect
Complete the chart to list causes and effects of the agricultural revolution.

Cause	→	Effect
	→	
	→	
	→	

New York Academic Content Standards
2.2, 2.4, 3.2

The Beginning of Agriculture

A farmer in Pakistan uses a traditional plow.

Visual Preview

How did the development of agriculture change human life?

A People learned how to farm in the New Stone Age.

B Slowly, some people settled in one place and developed farming methods.

24

A THE RISE OF FARMING

Do you ever think about the food in your grocery store? How is this food grown? Who brings it to the market? How did farming begin?

No one knows when farming, or **agriculture**, began. Some scientists think it may have been about 9,000 years ago. We do know that people first grew crops that had been growing wild in their region.

The New Stone Age

By about 7000 B.C., some people had settled in villages along rivers and lakes where there was fertile, or rich, soil for farming. These people no longer had to hunt and gather food as earlier humans had. They still used stone tools, however, so this time is called the New Stone Age.

In time, farmers began to raise more crops than they could eat. This extra food is called a **surplus**. Having surplus food allowed some people to do things other than farming. These people **specialized**, or did only one particular job. For example, they made only tools or bricks or clothing.

People came to villages to trade whatever they had for products they needed. For example, a farmer would exchange his extra wheat for a pair of sandals. There was no money, so they traded products rather than cash. This kind of trade is called **barter**.

Imagine the excitement on market day! You would go with your parents to the nearest village. Your mother carries fresh cheeses, and your father has made strong wooden bows. They hope to trade for cloth to make warm capes. You see old friends, and you notice strangers who speak in languages you don't understand. They bring clay pots or tools or baskets to trade for products from your village.

QUICK CHECK

Cause and Effect How did the development of agriculture change human life?

Wheat and olive oil, stored in ceramic jars, were important parts of the ancient diet. ▶

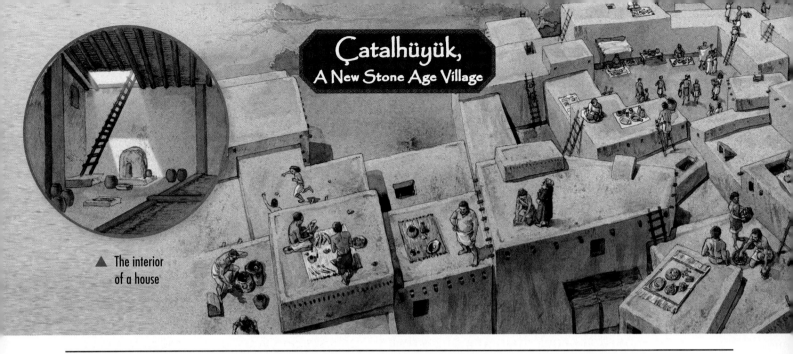

Çatalhüyük, A New Stone Age Village

▲ The interior of a house

B THE GROWTH OF FARMING

Farming gave people a steady diet, and they began to live longer. Populations grew, and villages became towns. Towns began to trade. People now had time to develop crafts and new ways of life.

Domesticating Animals and Plants

How did the early farmers get animals and crops? By the time people were living in small villages, they had learned to **domesticate** animals and wild plants. To domesticate means to raise something to be useful to people.

◀ A boy in traditional dress herds sheep in Iraq.

Scientists believe that the first domesticated animal was the dog. By around 14,000 B.C., some wild wolves had become domesticated dogs. Early farmers also domesticated goats, pigs, cattle, and sheep.

Farmers learned to domesticate wild plants as well, probably by trial and error, beginning with the grasses and fruits they liked best. One of the earliest crops seems to have been figs. Farmers also developed local grasses into wheat and rice crops.

Domesticating plants and animals caused a revolution, a great change in how people live or how things are done. Therefore, the change to farming in the New Stone Age is called the agricultural revolution.

Farming Techniques

Ancient people had to adapt their surroundings in order to farm. For example, they often built terraces, which are level platforms of earth that climb a hill like a staircase. In dry areas, they brought water to

▲ This interior view shows a temple.

Diagram Skill

How do you think people got into and out of their houses?

the crops through canals and reservoirs. In heavily forested areas, farmers cleared the land by "slash-and-burn." They cut down trees and bushes and burned the stumps and weeds.

Early people also studied the weather. Climate controlled the kinds of crops they could plant. For example, rice needs heavy rains and heat, while corn grows well in more temperate regions.

Tools for Farmers

Ancient people also developed new tools for farming. One of the most important was the adze, a kind of ax. The adze has a flat, carved stone head and was used to clear forests. Early farmers also developed the hoe for keeping weeds out of gardens and the sickle for cutting fields of grain.

QUICK CHECK

Cause and Effect How did farmers improve the way they did their work?

Check Understanding

1. **VOCABULARY** Write a paragraph about the New Stone Age. Use these vocabulary words in your paragraph.

   agriculture   specialize   domesticate
   surplus   barter

2. **READING SKILL Cause and Effect** Use your completed chart from page 24 to write a short summary of the information in the lesson.

Cause	→	Effect
	→	
	→	
	→	

 3. **Write About It** Write about how geography affected the farming methods and the crops of New Stone Age farmers.

Lesson 3

VOCABULARY

irrigation p. 30

city-state p. 32

polytheism p. 32

empire p. 32

scribe p. 33

READING SKILL

Cause and Effect

How did advances in farming affect life in Mesopotamia?

Cause	→	Effect
	→	
	→	
	→	

New York Academic Content Standards

2.1, 2.2, 2.3, 3.1

THE FERTILE CRESCENT

The Euphrates River in Iraq

Visual Preview

How did geography affect civilizations in the Fertile Crescent?

A An early farming civilization arose in Mesopotamia.

B Mesopotamians farmed by controlling local rivers.

C To keep records, the Sumerians created a writing system.

A ⓐ THE LAND BETWEEN THE RIVERS

In a region full of harsh deserts, people discovered that they could farm in the fertile plain between two rivers. They had to live with the risk of floods, but here they could settle and build communities.

One of the world's first farming communities developed in the Fertile Crescent in Asia. This rainbow-shaped strip of land lies between the Tigris and Euphrates Rivers and along their banks. It curves northward from the Persian Gulf and then dips southwest along the Mediterranean Sea. The Greeks would later call this region Mesopotamia, or "the land between the rivers." Today we call this part of Southwest Asia the Middle East.

The Tigris and Euphrates Rivers each begin as melting snow high in Turkey's Taurus Mountains. Each flows southeast and then empties into the Persian Gulf. The area's climate is usually hot and dry, and the rains are unpredictable. When there is little rain, parts of the rivers dry up, and crops can die. If there is heavy rainfall, the rivers can overflow, drowning crops and destroying homes. But when the rivers have their regular spring floods, they leave behind rich, fertile soil called silt.

The two rivers were extremely important to the early people of Mesopotamia. The rivers were the only source of water for drinking, farming,

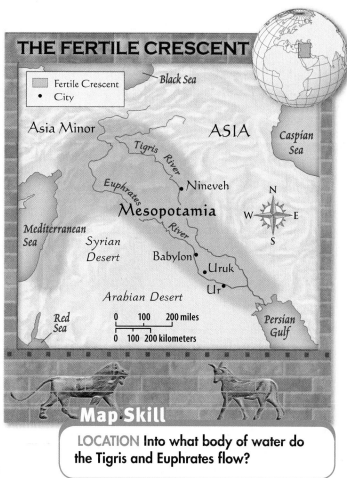

THE FERTILE CRESCENT

- Fertile Crescent
- • City

Black Sea
Asia Minor
ASIA
Tigris River
Nineveh
Euphrates River
Mesopotamia
Caspian Sea
Mediterranean Sea
Syrian Desert
Babylon
Uruk
Ur
Arabian Desert
Red Sea
Persian Gulf

0   100   200 miles
0   100   200 kilometers

Map Skill

LOCATION **Into what body of water do the Tigris and Euphrates flow?**

and washing. The Mesopotamians were one of the first groups of people to pray to gods for rain and good crops.

QUICK CHECK

Cause and Effect How did the Tigris and Euphrates Rivers affect the people of Mesopotamia?

Tigris River

Levee

Artificial lake

B LIFE IN MESOPOTAMIA

It took centuries, but Mesopotamian farmers eventually learned how to direct the water of the Tigris and Euphrates where they needed it. They used **irrigation,** or the bringing of water to dry fields by using canals or pipes. Farmers worked together to build canals. They also constructed dams to collect water in ponds for storage. To prevent flooding, they built high walls of dirt called levees along riverbanks. Managing the water supply was so important to early farmers that some of Mesopotamia's first laws dealt with sharing water fairly.

Their growing skill at controlling the Tigris and Euphrates made Mesopotamia's farmers some of the best farmers in the ancient world. Working their fields with simple tools such as wooden plows and hoes with stone edges, they grew wheat, barley, dates, onions, and other crops.

Mesopotamians used their geography and resources to their advantage. In addition to using the rivers for farming, they caught fish in the rivers. The rivers also provided mud and reeds for building houses. Mesopotamia had few trees, so wood was a valuable resource.

Ziggurat

Irrigation canal

▲ Irrigation helped Mesopotamians grow crops and avoid floods. Cities rose near major farmlands.

People used wood to make plows and furniture, as well as a new invention—the potter's wheel. As the wheel spun, a potter could mold lumps of clay into bowls and pots. Pottery soon became one of Mesopotamia's many art forms.

Animals Go to Work

Mesopotamian farmers also discovered how to raise animals for food and other goods. Sheep were among the first domesticated animals. They supplied meat as well as wool for clothing. Cattle were raised for their meat and their skins, which were made into leather. Farmers also trained them to carry goods and to pull plows. Mesopotamians tamed dogs, pigs, goats, and donkeys as well.

Trade and Crafts

The combination of rich soil, hard work, and new irrigation techniques helped Mesopotamians produce a surplus of crops. This surplus led to the growth of trade. Farmers would travel to nearby villages to exchange surplus grain and meat for things they needed. Surplus food also allowed people to specialize in crafts, like making baskets, cloth, and pottery. Villages became centers of trading and crafting.

QUICK CHECK

Cause and Effect How did geography affect the way people lived in Mesopotamia?

C CIVILIZATION IN SUMER

By 3000 B.C., Mesopotamia's villages had grown into larger cities, some with as many as 10,000 people. Many of these cities developed in southern Mesopotamia, near the Persian Gulf. This region became known as Sumer.

Sumer had dozens of large **city-states**—cities that had their own governments. The city-states developed strict social class systems, in which certain groups of people always held the same positions in society. At the top were kings, priests, and government officials. Below them were farmers, traders, and craftspeople. Enslaved people were the lowest class.

Religion in Sumer

Sumerians also practiced **polytheism**, or the belief in many gods and goddesses. Their gods included An, the father of the gods, and Inanna, the goddess of love and war. Another important god was Enki, the god of water.

The main building in each Sumerian city was a ziggurat, or "mountain of god." A temple honoring one of Sumer's gods stood at the top of each ziggurat. Sumerians believed their priests and priestesses could communicate with the gods and goddesses from the ziggurats.

The Sumerian Empire

For many years, Sumer's most powerful city-states tried to conquer each other and create an **empire**, a group of different lands under one ruler. Around 2300 B.C., Sargon, king of the city-state of Akkad, succeeded. He united Sumer under his rule, creating the first empire in world history.

Sargon ruled for about 56 years. After his death, his empire fell apart, as states from northern Mesopotamia attacked Sumer.

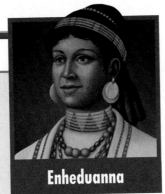

PEOPLE

Enheduanna, the daughter of Sargon, was a high priestess and the region's first known poet. In one poem she promised a goddess that, "I, Enheduanna, will offer prayers to her / My tears like sweet drinks, / Will I present to the holy Inanna. . . ."

Enheduanna

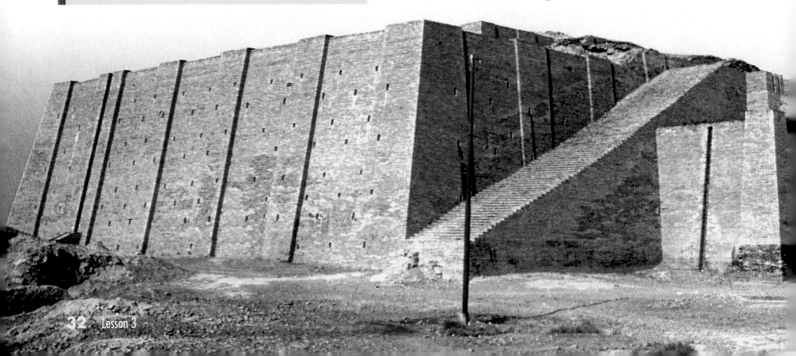

Sumerian Inventions

The Sumerians made discoveries that would influence other civilizations for centuries. Most important was the development of a writing system. Sumerians used cuneiform, or wedge-shaped marks, to record laws and important events. These marks were pressed into wet clay tablets with sharpened reeds. The tablets were then baked in the sun until dry. Some Sumerian tablets have survived until today.

Sumerians opened schools called edubbas, or "tablet houses." There, wealthy boys studied math and music and spent long days learning how to read and write cuneiform. Some would become official record-keepers, or **scribes**, who were highly respected.

Along with irrigation systems and pottery, the Sumerians invented or improved the wagon wheel and the sailboat. They also developed new systems of measurements. They were the first people to come up with a 12-month calendar. They used it to predict floods and decide the best times to plant crops. They also created the 60-second minute and the 60-minute hour—methods we still use to tell time today, more than 4,500 years later.

▼ This cuneiform tablet is a record of fields and crops from 2800 B.C.

QUICK CHECK

Cause and Effect How did Sumerian inventions affect life in Mesopotamia?

Check Understanding

1. **VOCABULARY** Use these vocabulary words to write a travel guide about ancient Sumer.

   city-state   empire
   polytheism   scribe

2. **READING SKILL Cause and Effect** Use your chart from page 28 to explain how advances in farming affected life in Mesopotamia.

 3. **Write About It** Write about how the Tigris and Euphrates Rivers affected life in the Fertile Crescent.

◀ The partially restored Third Sumerian Dynasty ziggurat in Ur, originally built around 2100 B.C.

BABYLONIA, ISRAEL, AND ASSYRIA

VOCABULARY

code p. 35

covenant p. 36

monotheism p. 36

astronomy p. 39

READING SKILL

Cause and Effect

Why did the Chaldeans lose power?

Cause	→	Effect
	→	
	→	
	→	

New York Academic Content Standards

2.1, 2.2, 2.3, 3.1

The Ishtar Gate in Babylon

Visual Preview

Why did empires rise and fall in Mesopotamia?

A By 1792 B.C., Babylonian king Hammurabi built an empire in Mesopotamia.

B The roots of Judaism can be traced to ancient Israel.

C By 650 B.C., Assyria built the largest empire the region had ever seen.

Ⓐ THE BABYLONIANS

They came to Mesopotamia as wandering herders and decided to settle in the city-state of Babylon, just north of the old Sumerian Empire. These former herders began to follow the customs of the local people, and their city grew strong. Eventually, they were ready to conquer.

Almost 500 years after the fall of Sumer, King Hammurabi of Babylon conquered Mesopotamian city-states north and south of his home. By 1792 B.C., he controlled the entire region—an empire several times larger than Sumer.

Hammurabi established a system of laws in his empire. There was no excuse for breaking Hammurabi's laws—for perhaps the first time in history, this king had them written down for everyone to read.

▲ This carving shows Hammurabi before the sun god.

Hammurabi's Code

The Code of Hammurabi was written down by scribes in about 1780 B.C. A **code** is a written collection of laws. The Code of Hammurabi is the oldest set of laws archaeologists have ever found. It listed 282 laws everyone in the empire had to follow—including the king. The code dealt with all parts of life, including crimes, farming and business activities, marriage, and the family. Several laws protected weaker people from the more powerful. Other laws set punishments that would probably seem cruel today. The laws were, however, typical of societies at that time. For example:

"If a man put out the eye of another man, his eye shall be put out.... If a son has struck his father, they shall cut off his hand."

As with Sumer, Hammurabi's empire came to an end. After Hammurabi's death, neighboring states conquered different pieces of his empire until it vanished. It would be 1,000 years before a new empire arose in Mesopotamia.

QUICK CHECK

Cause and Effect How did Hammurabi's code affect Mesopotamian civilization?

About 1000 B.C., a group of people called the Israelites built a kingdom in Canaan. Canaan was the region of Southwest Asia located at the eastern end of the Mediterranean Sea. Although the Israelite population was small, the religion they practiced became very influential. The Israelites were the first people in the world to practice **monotheism**—the belief in only one God. The Israelite faith eventually became known as Judaism, and the people who follow it became known as Jews.

The Israelites spoke a language called Hebrew and wrote down their history and religious beliefs in a collection of books known today as the Hebrew Bible. The Hebrew Bible is our major source for the early history of the Israelites.

Abraham and Moses

The history of the Israelites began about 1800 B.C., when according to the Hebrew Bible, God made a **covenant,** or special agreement, with a man named Abraham. Under this agreement, Abraham left his home in Mesopotamia and moved his family to Canaan. Once there, Abraham had a grandson named Jacob. Jacob was also called Israel, and this is why his descendents became known as Israelites. According to the Hebrew Bible, Jacob raised 12 sons. Each went on to form a separate tribe, or family group. They became known as the 12 tribes of Israel.

A drought forced the Israelites to move to Egypt, where the Egyptians enslaved them. Several hundred years later, according to the Hebrew Bible, God told an Israelite named Moses to lead his people out of Egypt. This escape from slavery is remembered by Jews each year during the celebration of Passover.

Ancient Israel

Sidon
Tyre
Samaria
Jerusalem
Jordan River
Mediterranean Sea
Dead Sea
N
W E
S
0 25 50 miles
0 25 50 kilometers
EGYPT
Gulf of Suez
SINAI
Kingdom of Israel
Kingdom of Judah

An archaeological dig at the site of the ancient Jewish temple in Jerusalem ▼

While the Israelites wandered in the desert on their way to Canaan, the Hebrew Bible says God gave Moses a set of laws. These are called the Torah. Among them are ten major rules known as the Ten Commandments.

The Kingdom of Israel

After Moses died, a leader named Joshua led the Israelites into Canaan, where they founded the Kingdom of Israel. In about 1000 B.C., a soldier named David became Israel's king. His capital, Jerusalem, became the kingdom's religious and political center. David's son, King Solomon, built a great temple in Jerusalem that became the center of religious life for Israelites.

After Solomon's death, Israel split into a northern kingdom called Israel and a southern kingdom called Judah. In 721 B.C., the Assyrians conquered the northern kingdom and scattered many Israelites across their empire. The kingdom of Judah survived, however, and this is why the Israelite religion became known as Judaism, and its followers became known as Jews.

Judah and the Diaspora

The Jews maintained their independence for another century, but beginning about 620 B.C., they came under the rule of a series of empires. First the Egyptians conquered them, followed by the Chaldeans, Persians, and Greeks.

Under Greek rule, some Jews continued to live in Judah. Others spread across the Greek empire. The Jews living outside Judah became known as the Diaspora, a word that means "scattered." They translated the Hebrew Bible into Greek. This version helped spread Jewish ideas throughout the Mediterranean world. In 167 B.C., the Jews rebelled against the Greeks and reestablished their kingdom, only to have it be conquered again a century later by the Romans in 63 B.C.

QUICK CHECK

Make Inferences How did the religion of the Israelites differ from others in the Fertile Crescent?

Primary Sources

1. I am the Lord your God who brought you out of the land of Egypt.

2. You shall have no other gods besides Me.

3. You shall not swear falsely by the name of the Lord your God.

4. Remember the sabbath day (weekly day of rest) and keep it holy.

5. Honor your father and your mother.

6. You shall not murder.

7. You shall not commit adultery.

8. You shall not steal.

9. You shall not bear false witness against (lie about) your neighbor.

10. You shall not covet (desire) . . . anything that is your neighbor's.

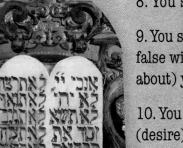

**from Exodus Chapter 20
The Hebrew Bible**

Write About It What do you think is commanded by the first commandment?

THE ASSYRIANS AND CHALDEANS

The Mesopotamian city-state of Ashur, with its fertile farmlands, had always been an attractive target for invaders. To defend themselves, the city's people—the Assyrians—formed a large army. By 900 B.C., that army had grown so strong that it began conquering its neighbors.

The Assyrian Empire

Assyrian soldiers were experts with the bow and arrow and were among the first fighters to use horse-drawn chariots in battle. Using new metalworking techniques, they created iron weapons that easily cut through weaker weapons made of bronze.

When the Assyrians attacked a city, they often tunneled under its walls or used tree trunks as battering rams to knock down its gates.

This copy of the Ishtar Gate can be seen in Iraq. ▼

Once inside the city, they burned its buildings, stole its valuables, and carried its people away. By 650 B.C., Assyria controlled the largest empire the region had ever seen—from the Persian Gulf, through the Fertile Crescent, and into Egypt. Assyrian kings divided their territory into smaller states known as provinces. They built new roads to help their soldiers get around more easily. The roads also made trade easier, which increased the empire's wealth.

Although the Assyrians destroyed the ancient city of Babylon, they built their own spectacular temples and palaces. They also constructed one of the world's first libraries, in their capital, Nineveh. Historians think it held about 25,000 cuneiform tablets with stories of the Assyrian gods.

Assyria's kings built a mighty empire, but the people they ruled hated them and hoped to rebel. Finally, in around 650 B.C., rebels attacked, and in 612 B.C., Nineveh—and the empire—fell.

The Chaldeans

The Chaldeans led this overthrow of Assyria and soon took control of Mesopotamia themselves. Under King Nebuchadnezzar, the Chaldeans rebuilt Babylon as a glorious new capital city surrounded by massive brick walls. A feature of the city was the Hanging Gardens, an area at the king's palace full of beautiful plants. One of the city's major entrances, the Ishtar Gate, was covered in shining blue tiles. A 300-foot-high ziggurat to Marduk, the chief god of Babylonia, towered over the city.

▲ Assyrian warriors march and ride chariots into battle.

The Chaldeans made major discoveries in **astronomy**, the study of the stars and planets. They followed the movement of the planets, made maps of the stars, and used what they learned to create an accurate calendar.

When Nebuchadnezzar died in 562 B.C., the empire was struggling. Building projects had used up much of the Chaldeans' wealth, and food shortages had weakened the people. In 539 B.C., Persia conquered Babylon. Persia's ruler, Cyrus the Great, allowed the Jews, who had been prisoners in Babylon, to return to their homeland. Judah and the rest of Mesopotamia now made up just one part of Cyrus's much larger territory.

QUICK CHECK

Cause and Effect How did Assyria's harsh rule weaken the empire?

Check Understanding

1. **VOCABULARY** Use the following words in a paragraph about the development of Judaism.

   code   covenant   monotheism

2. **READING SKILL Cause and Effect** Use your chart from page 34 to explain why the Chaldeans lost power.

Cause	→	Effect
	→	
	→	
	→	

 3. Write About It How did roads help Assyria?

The KINGDOMS of EGYPT

VOCABULARY

pharaoh p. 42

dynasty p. 42

hieroglyphics p. 44

papyrus p. 44

READING SKILL

Sequence Events
Complete this chart with important events in the history of ancient Egypt.

First
Next
Last

New York Academic Content Standards
2.1, 2.2, 2.3, 2.4, 3.1

The temple of Amon at Luxor, Egypt

Visual Preview

Why was ancient Egypt able to remain a great power for centuries?

A Life in Egypt is the "Gift of the Nile."

B Egyptian history is divided into three kingdoms.

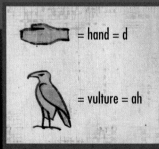

= hand = d

= vulture = ah

C The Egyptians developed a writing system.

THE GIFT OF THE NILE

In ancient times, there were actually two Egypts. Upper Egypt began at the cataracts, or rock-filled rapids in southern Egypt. Lower Egypt, to the north, included the lowlands of the Nile Delta.

Deserts! Cataracts! It might seem that geography was hard on Egypt. Actually, geography helped the Egyptians. First, the Nile River was a water "highway" for travel. Also, harsh deserts prevented attacks from the east or west.

The Annual Flood

The Nile River begins in the highlands of Africa, south of Egypt. Every summer heavy rains pour down on the highlands and run off into the Nile. The rainwaters carry off rich topsoil from the highlands. Nile floods carry this topsoil to Egypt each summer. The timing of the floods could be predicted, but the size of the floods could not. Some years, less rain meant smaller floods and less rich topsoil. Other years, heavy rains caused destructive floods. No wonder Hapi, the Nile god, and Khnemu, the flood god, were two of the most important gods of ancient Egypt!

Using Mathematics

Each year, Nile floodwaters covered fields and villages. After floodwaters ran off, Egyptians had to figure out which farmer owned which land. The Egyptians used a kind of mathematics called geometry to locate each farmer's field. You may be using geometry in your math classes today!

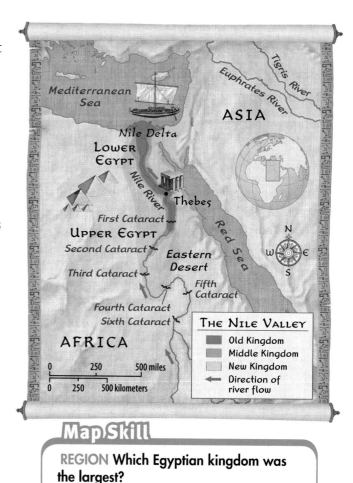

Map Skill

REGION **Which Egyptian kingdom was the largest?**

QUICK CHECK

Sequence Events Describe the series of events that happen when the Nile River floods.

The history of ancient Egypt is often divided into three time periods, beginning with the Old Kingdom (c. 3100 to 2200 B.C.). Next came the Middle Kingdom (c. 2100 to 1700 B.C.). The last was the New Kingdom (c. 1500 to 1000 B.C.).

The Pharaoh's Rule

About 3100 B.C., the ruler of Upper Egypt conquered Lower Egypt and created one kingdom, which historians call the Old Kingdom. No one is sure of its first ruler's name. He is often called Menes, and he was the first **pharaoh.** The word pharaoh means "great house" or "palace." Eventually, the word came to mean the rulers themselves. Pharaohs controlled Egyptian life for the next 2,000 years!

As the Old Kingdom came to an end, Egypt's rulers were weak. For about a century, many different people were in charge for short periods of time. Then, around 2100 B.C., a new set of rulers emerged.

The Middle Kingdom

These new rulers were all from the same ruling family, or **dynasty.** During the Middle Kingdom, Egyptian armies made Egypt into an empire.

The Middle Kingdom ended when an enemy with new technology appeared. The Hyksos, a group of people from western Asia, had horses and chariots whereas the Egyptians had only donkey carts. The Hyksos also had better bows and arrows and battle axes. The Hyksos armies took over Egypt around 1650 B.C.

TIME LINE OF EGYPT'S PHARAOHS

3100 B.C.   **1600 B.C.**   **1500 B.C.**

3100 B.C. Menes unites Egypt and becomes the first pharaoh.

1503 B.C. Hatshepsut, the first female pharaoh, begins to rule.

The New Kingdom

About 1550 B.C., Pharaoh Ahmose I used the Hyksos technology to arm his soldiers. His army defeated the Hyksos and established the New Kingdom. Once again, Egypt ruled a large empire, including the Fertile Crescent.

Unusual Rulers

One New Kingdom pharaoh was a woman! Hatshepsut began to rule in 1503 B.C. after the death of her husband. While she ruled, Egypt was peaceful and grew rich from trade.

In 1379 B.C., Egypt had another unusual pharaoh. Egyptians worshipped many gods, but Amenhotep IV worshipped only one god, called Aten. The pharaoh changed his name to Akhenaton to honor Aten. He angered the priests and followers of other gods. After his death, his hated name was removed from temples and other monuments.

Ramses II was the last great Egyptian pharaoh. He ruled for 67 years. Ramses moved Egypt's capital to the Nile Delta, and he built a gigantic rock temple at Abu Simbel, in Upper Egypt. After his death the New Kingdom began a gradual decline and ended around 1000 B.C.

QUICK CHECK

Cause and Effect **What effect did new weapon technology have on the Middle Kingdom?**

1400 B.C.	1300 B.C.	1200 B.C.
1350 B.C. Akhenaton tries to make Egyptians worship one god.	**1336** B.C. Nefertiti, wife of Akhenaton, disappears from history.	**1213** B.C. Ramses II, Egypt's greatest pharaoh, leaves many monuments.

C WRITING WITH PICTURES

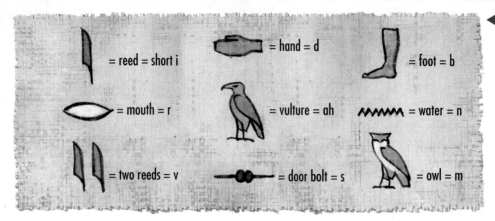

= reed = short i

= hand = d

= foot = b

= mouth = r

= vulture = ah

= water = n

= two reeds = v

= door bolt = s

= owl = m

◄ Each of these hieroglyphics represents a sound. How would you write the name of the first pharaoh?

For more than 3,000 years, the ancient Egyptians wrote with **hieroglyphics.** Hieroglyphics are pictures or symbols that represent ideas, sounds, or objects. They were carved and painted on walls and monuments.

Scribes controlled this writing system, which Egyptians called "the words of God." The scribes taught hieroglyphics to students. Almost always boys, these students started school at the age of ten. Learning hieroglyphics took many years.

Egyptians developed a kind of paper called **papyrus.** The papyrus reed plant grows along the Nile River. Scribes used sharp papyrus reed stems to make pens for writing on papyrus rolls.

Breaking the Code

The meaning of hieroglyphics was lost for many years. About two centuries ago, a Frenchman discovered how to read the pictures. Historians and archaeologists learned a great deal about the daily life of ancient Egypt once they were able to read the hieroglyphic writing. Even though we no longer write with hieroglyphics, we still use an Egyptian writing term. Our word "paper" comes from the Egyptian word "papyrus."

QUICK CHECK

Compare and Contrast How are hieroglyphics like and unlike the alphabet used in English?

Check Understanding

1. **VOCABULARY** Write a paragraph describing a trip back in time to ancient Egypt using the following vocabulary words.

   pharaoh   hieroglyphics
   dynasty   papyrus

2. **READING SKILL Sequence Events** Use your chart from page 40 to make a time line of events between 3100 B.C. and 1000 B.C.

   First
   ↓
   Next
   ↓
   Last

3. **Write About It** Describe how geography influenced ancient Egypt.

Map and Globe Skills

Use Topographic Maps

VOCABULARY

topographic map
elevation
contour

A **topographic map** is a physical map that shows the features of Earth's surface. Map colors may show **elevation**, the height of land above sea level. The maps use **contours**, imaginary lines that enclose areas of equal elevation. Numbers inside the contours identify the height at the boundary of each contour. Follow the steps to learn how to use topographic maps.

Learn It

Identify the map on this page by its title.

● The map key tells you what each color means. What color are lands at sea level?

● The key also uses symbols. What is the symbol for a mountain peak?

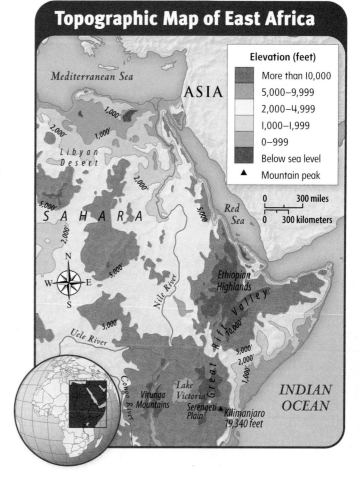

Try It

Use the map to answer the following questions.

● What is the height of the mountain on this topographic map?

● Why do contours have numbers on a topographical map?

● What is the elevation of the Ethiopian Highlands?

Apply It

● Describe how the elevation changes as you travel from the Mediterranean Sea to Mount Kilimanjaro.

● What information about northeast Africa can you not learn from a topographic map?

Lesson 6

VOCABULARY

mummy p. 49

pyramid p. 50

READING SKILL

Cause and Effect
Complete the chart to show how Egyptian beliefs made them plan carefully for life after death.

Cause	→	Effect
	→	
	→	
	→	

New York Academic Content Standards
2.1, 2.2, 2.3, 2.4, 3.1, 4.1

THE CULTURE OF EGYPT

A pharaoh's golden burial mask

Visual Preview

What made Egyptian culture unique?

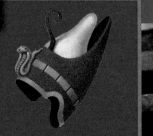

A Egypt had a farming economy directed by the pharaoh.

B Much of Egypt's culture centered on life after death.

C Egyptians made advances in mathematics and science.

Ⓐ EGYPT'S ECONOMY

If someone offers you an ancient Egyptian coin, don't take it! The ancient Egyptians had no coins. In fact, they had no money at all!

Although ancient Egyptians did not use money, Egypt had a strong economy. An economy is the way a country's goods and services are produced and distributed. Most modern economies are a combination of agriculture and manufacturing.

Ancient Egypt's long growing season led to an economy based on agriculture. Its major products were barley and emmer, a type of wheat. Egyptians were also experts in glassmaking, metalwork, and pottery.

Since ancient Egypt had no coins or money, Egyptians had to barter. You have already learned that barter means to trade goods without the use of money. An economy that does not use money is called a barter economy. Egyptians sent some of their extra crops to other countries and traded them for luxury goods and other products. Any additional crops and supplies were stored in large warehouses in case of need.

The pharaoh ordered a tax on everything made or grown in Egypt. Since Egyptians did not use money, the pharaoh collected a part of every farmer's crops as a tax, as well as a portion of products such as leather goods, linen cloth, and baskets. The pharaoh's taxes also included days

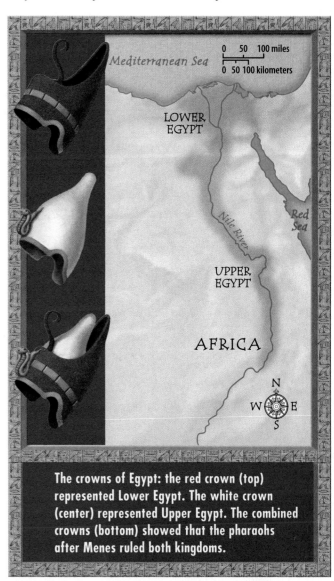

The crowns of Egypt: the red crown (top) represented Lower Egypt. The white crown (center) represented Upper Egypt. The combined crowns (bottom) showed that the pharaohs after Menes ruled both kingdoms.

of work. Almost all Egyptians worked on government building projects during the flood season.

QUICK CHECK

Cause and Effect What caused people to barter in ancient Egypt?

47

B LIFE AFTER DEATH

Egyptians believed they would have a new life after they died. They made elaborate preparations for this life after death.

Egyptians developed a way to preserve the dead with minerals and special spices, called resins. The body was then wrapped in

THE MUMMY CASE

The mummy was buried in a decorated box called a mummy case. Most of these boxes were painted wood, with pictures of gods and secret prayers painted on the sides. ▶

FOR THE NEXT LIFE ▲

Egyptian tombs included everything a person would need in the next life. Items included clothing, food, weapons, and even games. The game above is called *senet*. Can you figure out rules to play this game?

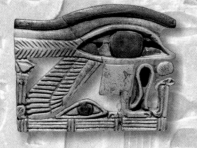

INSIDE THE MUMMY ▲

The Egyptians used charms, called amulets, to protect the mummy. These amulets were wrapped in the linen coverings. This amulet is called "the eye of Horus."

long strips of linen. The wrapped body is called a **mummy**. It could take a few days to more than two months to prepare a mummy. The dry air of the Egyptian desert has helped to preserve many of these mummies.

QUICK CHECK

Cause and Effect Why did Egyptians work so hard to prepare the dead?

ORGAN JARS

The liver, lungs, stomach, and intestines were removed and carefully preserved in special jars, called canopic jars. The mummy would need these organs in the next life. ▼

A GOD OF THE DEAD

The Egyptians believed that the goddess Isis made the first mummy. During the ceremony of making a mummy, the chief priest wore a dog mask of Anubis, a god of the dead. ▶

DataGraphic

Reading Hieroglyphics

Chart A shows a list of items that were left in one tomb. The list is written in hieroglyphics. Chart B shows the symbols for writing numbers in ancient Egypt.

Chart A

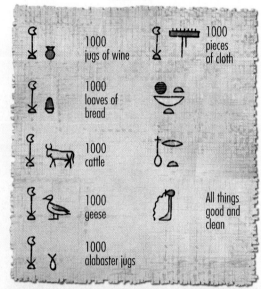

1000 jugs of wine

1000 pieces of cloth

1000 loaves of bread

1000 cattle

1000 geese

All things good and clean

1000 alabaster jugs

Chart B

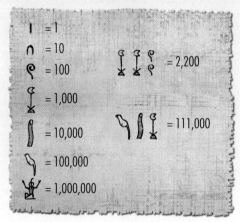

| = 1

∩ = 10

= 100

= 1,000

= 2,200

= 10,000

= 111,000

= 100,000

= 1,000,000

Think About the Hieroglyphics

If the bread was packed in ten baskets, how many loaves would there be in each? Write your answer in Egyptian numbers.

49

Egyptians worshipped many gods. There were gods for farming and crafts, for the Nile flood, and for the sun. Every city and town also had local gods.

The most important god was Ra, the sun god and the source of all life. The pharaoh was believed to be a child of Ra, and in turn, a god also. Another important Egyptian goddess was Isis, who protected people from sickness and harm.

A Pharaoh's Tomb

The Egyptians built many large temples and palaces. They also built enormous stone tombs called **pyramids**. These mountains of stone were the burial places of the early pharaohs. The best known pyramids are at Giza on the west bank of the Nile River, near modern Cairo.

The largest one is the Great Pyramid of Pharaoh Khufu. It contains more than two million stone blocks and is the largest pyramid in the world. The base covers 13 acres, an area almost as large as ten football fields. This gigantic pyramid took about 20 years to complete. Men worked on it for three to four months each year, while the Nile floodwaters covered their fields.

Egyptian Advances

Ancient Egyptians were great engineers and builders. Within Egypt, they built canals and dams for irrigation, which increased the amount of land they could farm. They even built a canal for trade between the Nile River and the Red Sea.

▲ Pyramids in Egypt

pyramid

tombs for royal family

EVENT

In 1954, Egyptian **archaeologists found a wooden boat** buried near the Great Pyramid. The boat was rebuilt and is on display in a Cairo museum.

Khufu's boat

Egypt was a leader in mathematics in the ancient world. You have already read about the Egyptians' use of geometry. They also developed methods for measuring weights, areas, lengths, and distances. Egyptians worked with a base ten system, and they created fractions that they used with whole numbers to add, subtract, and divide.

Egyptian astronomers identified the five planets in our solar system that can be seen without a telescope. Egyptians also combined mathematics and astronomy to develop a calendar with 12 months and 365 days.

Egyptian doctors learned about the human body. They were able to check a patient's pulse and heartbeat for signs of illness. They could set broken bones and sew wounds closed. They even performed brain surgery!

Scribes wrote medical papers to train other doctors. These papers described early antibiotics. Doctors covered infections with moldy bread or honey, which are natural sources of antibiotics. Egyptian dentists were able to fill cavities.

QUICK CHECK

Cause and Effect How did Egyptians increase the amount of land they could farm?

Check Understanding

1. **VOCABULARY** Write a sentence that explains the meaning of each word.

   mummy   **pyramid**

2. **READING SKILL Cause and Effect** Use your chart from page 46 to explain why Egyptians prepared so carefully for death.

3. **Write About It** Write about the relationship between Egypt's geographical location and its culture.

funeral temple

51

Early Indian Civilizations

VOCABULARY

monsoon p. 53

deity p. 56

reincarnation p. 56

artisan p. 56

caste p. 57

READING SKILL

Cause and Effect
Complete this chart with
the causes and effects of
the rise of the Indus River
Valley civilization.

Cause	→	Effect
	→	
	→	
	→	

**New York Academic
Content Standards**
2.1, 2.2, 2.3, 3.1, 3.2

Ruins of Mohenjo-Daro

Visual Preview

What influenced the development of early Indian culture?

A The Indus River and monsoons influenced Indian life.

B The Indus Valley civilization developed trading cities.

C Hinduism influenced Indian life and culture.

A   THE GEOGRAPHY OF INDIA

India is separated from the rest of Asia by tall mountains. India, Nepal, Bhutan, Bangladesh, Pakistan, and the island nations of Sri Lanka and Maldives make up the region called South Asia.

Look at the map on this page. You can see that India hangs out like a diamond from the continent of Asia. It is a subcontinent, a large landmass separated from the rest of a continent. The towering Himalaya to its north have some of the tallest mountains on Earth. For this reason, India developed a separate culture from much of the rest of Asia.

Two Rivers

The Ganges and Indus Rivers begin in the snowy Himalayan peaks. The Ganges River flows southeast to the Bay of Bengal. The Indus River flows southwest to the Arabian Sea, spreading fertile silt over the Indus Plain. South of these river valleys is the dry Deccan Plateau. However, there are lush, fertile plains along the east and west coasts of the subcontinent.

Seasonal Rains

A **monsoon** is a seasonal wind. In winter it blows west, bringing cool, dry air across the subcontinent. It reverses in summer and blows east, carrying warm, wet air and heavy rains to the subcontinent. The people of India depend on the monsoons, but the monsoons can also bring trouble. Too little rain brings drought. Too much rain brings floods. The monsoons have blown for centuries. About 3,000 years ago, farmers began to take advantage of this seasonal weather.

QUICK CHECK

Cause and Effect How can the seasonal winds cause trouble?

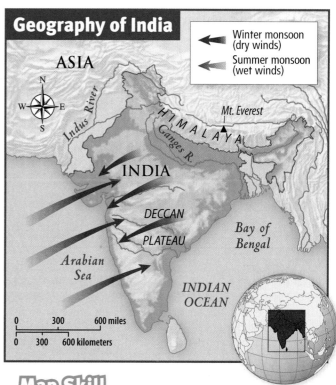

Geography of India

Winter monsoon (dry winds)
Summer monsoon (wet winds)

ASIA

Indus River

HIMALAYA

Mt. Everest

Ganges R.

INDIA

DECCAN PLATEAU

Bay of Bengal

Arabian Sea

INDIAN OCEAN

0   300   600 miles
0   300   600 kilometers

Map Skill

LOCATION In which season do the monsoon winds blow from the Arabian Sea to the east?

THE INDUS CIVILIZATION

Thousands of years ago, several rivers flowed through the Indus River region. Cities developed along these rivers. These cities grew and developed into a complex civilization called the Indus or Harappan civilization. Today two of these cities are called Harappa and Mohenjo-Daro, but we do not know what the people who lived there called them. They left a written language, but historians have not been able to read it yet.

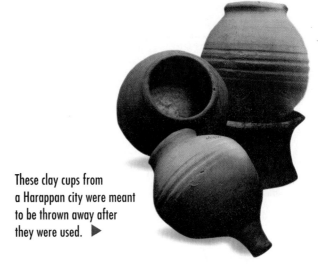

These clay cups from a Harappan city were meant to be thrown away after they were used. ▶

Society, Agriculture, and Culture

By studying artifacts, archaeologists have learned that Harappan civilization was well organized. It was ruled by priests or members of the merchant class. Religion and leadership seem to have been closely related.

Harappan farmers grew a variety of crops, including wheat, barley, and cotton. They also domesticated sheep, cattle, water buffalo, and pigs. Surplus food was dried and stored in case of a drought or a crop failure.

Artisans created toys, furnishings, and jewelry from wood, stone, and ivory. They made pots and tools from copper and bronze. There were also potters, who made vases and statues from clay. Other artisans wove cloth or carved stone into statues and other objects.

MOHENJO-DARO

Shops

Paved street

▲ Harappan artifacts include toys like this wheeled cart and the game board on the right.

The larger Harappan cities had as many as 35,000 people. They became centers of trade because people from other cultures were eager to trade for Harappan goods. Artifacts show that Harappan merchants traded with Mesopotamia and the people of Central Asia.

A Civilization Declines

Harappan civilization lasted more than 1,000 years. Historians are not sure why the cities of the Indus Valley declined. Some think that climate change brought floods or drought. Others believe an earthquake changed the course of the Indus River and caused the other rivers to dry up.

Some historians think the Harappan civilization might have ended because a new group of people moved into the region. This group, the Aryans, were hunters and herders who became farmers after they settled among the Harappans. All we know for certain, however, is that the Harappan cities slowly declined in wealth and importance and that people from other areas settled in the region.

QUICK CHECK

Cause and Effect What part might geography have played in ending the Harappan civilization?

Harappan cities had sewers, wide streets, trash collection, and even indoor bathrooms! Thousands of people lived in these well-planned cities. ▼

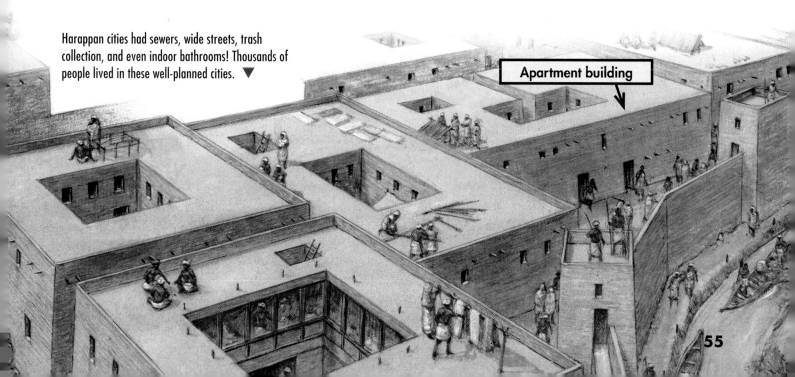

Apartment building

India is the birthplace of Hinduism, one of the world's oldest religions. Hindu beliefs developed on the Indian subcontinent over thousands of years. Today more than 830 million people in India are Hindus.

The Roots of Hinduism

The four Vedas, or "Books of Knowledge," are the oldest sacred texts of Hinduism. They contain hymns and prayers praising **deities**, or gods and goddesses.

Primary Sources

"As a great fish swims between the banks of a river as it likes, so does the shining self move between the states of dreaming and waking.

The self is beyond good and evil, beyond all the suffering of the human heart."

from the *Upanishads*, poetic writings about the Vedas

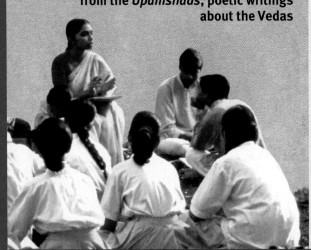

Write About It How does the self seem like a great fish?

These sacred texts survived as a moral history. Students listened and memorized the verses. For many centuries the Vedas were only spoken. Eventually the Vedas were written out in Sanskrit, the language in which they had been memorized.

Beliefs of Hinduism

Hindus believe that a soul survives death to be reborn in a new body. This rebirth is known as **reincarnation**. The soul carries karma from one life to the next. Karma is a force created by each person's good and bad acts.

The Caste System

Ancient India had four broad social classes called varnas. The Brahmins were priests and scholars. The Kshatriyas were warriors and rulers. The Vaisyas were **artisans**, or skilled workers, farmers, and merchants. The Sudras were servants and laborers.

Over time, a **caste** system developed within the varnas. A caste is a social group into which a person is born. There were thousands of castes. The caste system kept groups separate and set the rules for everyone's behavior.

A fifth group of people, called the Untouchables, was not part of the caste system. Members of this group performed the most undesirable tasks. Life for the Untouchable was hard. Most Indians believed that being near an Untouchable was harmful, so Untouchables were forced to live apart from others.

Each person in the caste system had duties, called dharma. The word *dharma* means, literally, "laws and duties." The duties are described in the Vedas.

QUICK CHECK

Summarize What are the Vedas?

Check Understanding

1. **VOCABULARY** Write a sentence for each vocabulary word below.

   monsoon   reincarnation   artisan
   deity   caste

2. **READING SKILL Cause and Effect** Use your completed chart to explain what may have led to the decline of the Harappan civilization.

Cause	→	Effect
	→	
	→	
	→	

3. **Write About It** How did geography lead to the growth of cities in India?

Among the Hindu deities are (from left) Brahma, the Creator; Vishnu, the Preserver; and Shiva, the Destroyer. ▼

VOCABULARY

raja p. 59

export p. 62

import p. 62

epic p. 62

READING SKILL

Cause and Effect
Use this chart to list the causes and effects of early empires in India.

Cause	→	Effect
	→	
	→	
	→	

New York Academic Content Standards
2.1, 2.2, 2.3, 3.1, 3.2

EARLY INDIAN EMPIRES

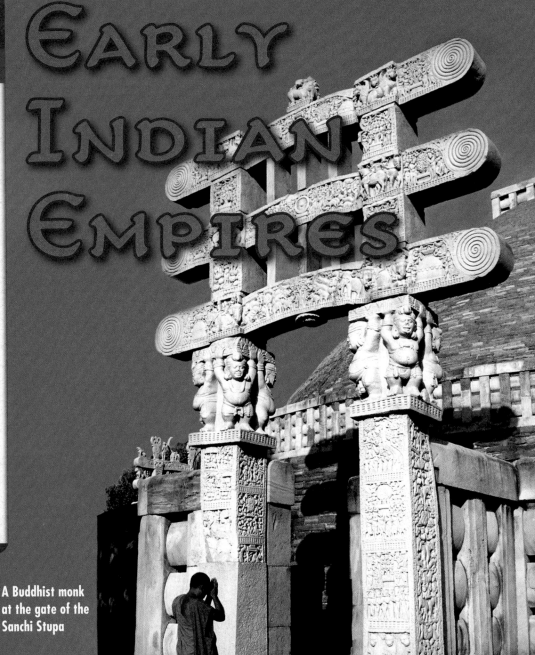

A Buddhist monk at the gate of the Sanchi Stupa

Visual Preview

How did religion affect government in early India?

A The Mauryan Empire was founded in 321 B.C.

B Siddhartha's teachings formed Buddhism.

C India had many cultural advances during the Gupta Empire.

THE FIRST INDIAN EMPIRE

*In about 321 B.C., an Indian **raja,** or ruler, named Chandragupta Maurya created an empire in the northern Indian subcontinent and central Asia. Maurya centralized his government so that he could rule his vast empire from his capital city, Pataliputra, in the Ganges River valley.*

Many of Maurya's ideas seem "modern" to us. Governments require money, so Maurya collected taxes to pay for his projects. He organized a postal system and ordered well-paved roadways so that he would be well informed about events inside his empire. His "Royal Highway" connected Pataliputra to the city of Taxila in northwest India. This road, called the Grand Trunk Road, is still in use today.

India's Greatest Emperor

Chandragupta Maurya's grandson, Asoka, became ruler in 273 B.C. One of the first things Asoka did was to attack another kingdom. Thousands of people were killed. Asoka was horrified. He became a Buddhist, and he gave up war.

Although Asoka was a Buddhist, he allowed his people to practice their own religions. His rule brought more than 40 years of peace and prosperity. India became a center of a trade network that reached as far as the Mediterranean world.

Many historians consider Asoka one of the most successful rulers of all time. After Asoka's death, later rulers were weak or poorly advised. The Mauryan Empire weakened and began to break apart. Around 185 B.C., it broke up into small kingdoms with local rulers.

QUICK CHECK

Cause and Effect What was the cause of Asoka's decision to avoid war?

A lion pillar erected by Asoka in Sarnath, India ▼

THE BUDDHA'S TEACHINGS

The religion of Buddhism had developed around 600 B.C. It began in a small kingdom in the Himalaya, in what today is Nepal. Buddhism spread across India because it promised ordinary Indians a simpler religion than Hinduism.

By the time Asoka began to rule India, Buddhism was widespread. It had followed trade routes into other parts of Asia. The story of Buddhism begins with the birth of a baby to a princely family.

Primary Sources

"He avoids the killing of living beings . . . . He avoids stealing, and avoids taking what is not given to him. . . . He lives with a heart honest and pure. . . . He avoids lying . . . . He speaks the truth, is devoted to the truth, reliable, worthy of confidence, no deceiver of men."

from the Eightfold Path, *The Word of the Buddha*

✏ **Write About It** What behaviors should be avoided?

The Story of a Prince

One night about 2,500 years ago, an Indian queen had a dream. She dreamed that her unborn child would be a great king, but only if he stayed with his family. If he left, he would become a great teacher. The queen told her husband about her dream. Shortly afterward she gave birth to a son, Siddhartha Gautama.

Siddhartha's father wanted the young prince to stay with his family. He filled the palace with beautiful things to please his son. The prince seemed to enjoy his life. He grew up surrounded by gardens and beautiful objects. He married and had a son.

Then one day he decided to leave the palace and explore the world. For the first time, he saw people in pain and suffering. Siddhartha wanted to find out why there was so much suffering in the world. Siddhartha left his father's palace and his young wife and son. He would spend years traveling around India trying to find out why people suffered.

Siddhartha began to meditate, or think deeply, about life. Once, he meditated for 49 days. Then, suddenly, he understood. He realized that people's suffering is caused by their desires. If people could get rid of their desires, they could end their suffering. Siddhartha shared his discovery with others. He became known as the Buddha, or "Enlightened One." To be enlightened means to have a special understanding. The Buddha's lessons are the foundation of Buddhism.

◄ The lotus is the Buddhist symbol of the search for enlightenment.

▲ A group of Buddhist monks in Thailand

The Four Noble Truths

The heart of the Buddha's teachings is called the Four Noble Truths:

1. Life is full of suffering.

2. People suffer because of their wants and needs.

3. The way to end suffering is to stop desiring things.

4. The way to stop one's desires is to follow the Eightfold Path.

The Eightfold Path

The Eightfold Path outlines a way to live according to the Buddha's teachings:

1. Know and understand the Four Noble Truths.

2. Give up worldly things, and don't harm others.

3. Tell the truth, don't gossip, and don't speak badly of others.

4. Don't commit evil acts, like killing, stealing, or living an unclean life.

5. Do rewarding work that does not involve harming any living thing.

6. Work for good and oppose evil.

7. Control your thoughts and feelings.

8. Practice meditation as a way of understanding reality.

According to the Buddha, the Eightfold Path is a practical way to free people from their desires and therefore achieve enlightenment. Buddhists believe that following the Path finally leads to understanding the truth about all things—a condition of wisdom called nirvana. Reverence for all life and a belief in reincarnation are also characteristics of Buddhism.

QUICK CHECK

Cause and Effect According to the Buddha, what was the cause of all suffering?

61

C THE GUPTA EMPIRE

▲ An illustration from the *Ramayana* shows the wedding procession of Rama.

A prince created the Gupta Empire in A.D. 320. Like an earlier ruler, his name was Chandragupta. His empire controlled northern India for about 200 years.

A New Empire

Chandragupta's son, Samudragupta, increased the power of the empire. He did not govern directly. He allowed defeated rulers to remain in power, but each had to pay tribute, a sort of yearly tax. Tribute payments helped make the Gupta Empire wealthy.

Chandragupta II was the son of Samudragupta. During his reign, salt, cotton, and spices were important Gupta **exports**. An export is a trade good sent out of a country. An **import** is a product brought into a country. Imports such as silk, pottery, copper, and glassware came into India from other countries.

Gupta Achievements

Two of India's greatest works of literature were written during the Gupta Empire. Both are sacred texts. The *Mahabharata* and the *Ramayana* are **epics**. An epic is a long poem that tells about the life of a hero. The *Mahabharata* contains a famous section called the *Bhagavad Gita*, or Song of the Lord.

The *Ramayana* tells about a great king named Rama and his faithful wife, Sita. The *Ramayana* is very popular in modern India. It is still performed often on stage and in movies.

One of the great contributions to mathematics came from the Gupta dynasty. The Indians of this period developed the decimal system, based on counting by tens. They devised the numerals from 1 to 9 that we use today. They also invented the zero and the idea of place value. Without a zero, none of our modern technology, such as computers, would be possible.

Indian mathematicians also invented algorithms, the steps that solve math problems. Computer programmers use algorithms to tell a computer what to do. A famous Indian mathematician, Aryabhata, was probably the first person to use algebra.

Indian astronomers made advancements as well. They discovered that the sun was the center of the solar system 1,000 years before European astronomers learned this. They also seem to have understood the idea of gravity.

Jain worshippers pray and offer fruit. ▼

Jainism

Jainism is another important Indian religion. Jainism was founded around 600 B.C., and wise teachers have revealed its truths throughout the centuries. Jainism teaches *ahimsa*, which is nonviolence toward humans and all other living things. You will read in Unit 6 how an Indian named Mohandas Gandhi used ahimsa to gain India's independence in the 1940s. Nonviolence changed American history as well. In the 1960s, Martin Luther King, Jr., used nonviolence during the American Civil Rights movement.

QUICK CHECK

Cause and Effect What effect did tribute payments have on the Gupta Empire?

Check Understanding

1. **VOCABULARY** Write a short summary of the Indian empires. Use each vocabulary word.

   raja   export   epic

2. **READING SKILL Cause and Effect** Use your chart to write about the effects of early empires on the history of India.

Cause	→	Effect
	→	
	→	
	→	

3. **Write About It** How did early Indian empires take advantage of local geography to grow and prosper?

EXPLORE The Big Idea

Lesson 9

VOCABULARY

loess p. 65

warlord p. 66

oracle p. 67

pictograph p. 67

READING SKILL

Cause and Effect

How did iron weapons change Chinese warfare?

Cause	→	Effect
	→	
	→	
	→	

New York Academic Content Standards
2.1, 2.2, 2.3, 3.1, 3.2

CHINA'S FIRST DYNASTIES

The Huang He (Yellow River) in China

Visual Preview

How did geography affect early Chinese civilization?

A Chinese civilization began in the Huang He valley.

B The Shang dynasty learned to control the Huang He.

C After a 200-year struggle for power, the state of Qin built the first Chinese empire.

A THE MIDDLE KINGDOM

*The villagers walked among the ruined homes, looking for survivors.
It had been the worst flood anyone could remember. Yet no one planned
to move away. Where would they go? What other place had better soil?*

On the Plateau of Tibet, a plain so high it's called "the roof of the world," a mighty river begins. It is the Huang He, and it flows 3,400 miles across northern China to the Yellow Sea. In Chinese, *Huang He* means Yellow River. Its name comes from the rich yellow soil called **loess** that the wind blows into its waters as it flows east. During the rainy summer season, huge amounts of loess wash into the Huang He, making it the muddiest river on Earth. When the river floods, it deposits this soil along its eastern banks. It is here that Chinese civilization began.

▲ This ancient map shows China at the center of the world.

Fighting the River

After farmers discovered they could grow crops in the valley, people moved there. They planted rice, wheat, and other crops. Farming along the Huang He has never been easy. The river often changes direction and floods the valley. Over the years, the Huang He has killed thousands, which is why it is also called "China's Sorrow."

Early Chinese farmers tried to control the flooding by building levees, but it did not always work. When a storm blew through, it sometimes carried the light, dusty loess away with it. This could destroy a harvest and leave families facing famine.

China's geography separated it from other civilizations. Mountain ranges like the Himalaya formed a high wall between China and the lands to the south and west. Few outsiders dared to cross the Taklimakan or Gobi deserts north of the Huang He. The Chinese called their land "the Middle Kingdom," and their maps put it right at the center of the Earth.

QUICK CHECK

Cause and Effect Why did Chinese civilization begin in the Huang He valley?

THE SHANG AND THE ZHOU

With the hard work of early Chinese farmers, strong communities grew in the Huang He valley. As people learned to store, or save, their surplus food, some Chinese began to specialize. Craftworkers, for example, began making pottery and bronze objects, some of which have survived until today.

The Shang Dynasty

Eventually, a powerful kingdom arose. Its rulers were known as the Shang dynasty, because the ruling family came from a state in the Shang valley. Using bronze weapons and horse-drawn chariots, Shang troops conquered neighboring states. They took charge of most of the Huang He valley by 1750 B.C.

The Shang probably built China's first cities, including their capital, Anyang. Shang kings chose **warlords**, military leaders who had their own armies, to rule the cities and other parts of the kingdom. Under the Shang, most Chinese people were farmers who worked on lands owned by nobles.

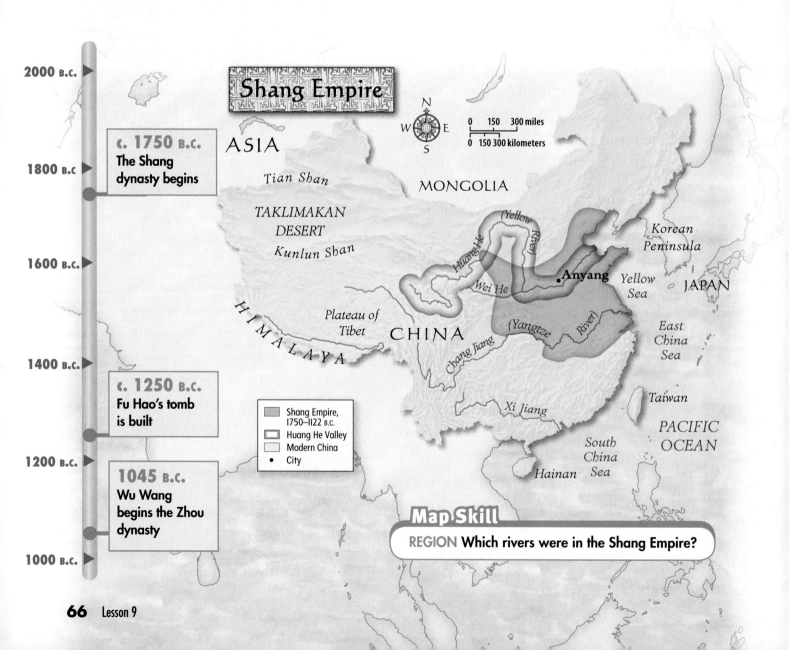

2000 B.C.

c. 1750 B.C.
The Shang dynasty begins

1800 B.C

1600 B.C.

1400 B.C.

c. 1250 B.C.
Fu Hao's tomb is built

1200 B.C.

1045 B.C.
Wu Wang begins the Zhou dynasty

1000 B.C.

Shang Empire

Shang Empire, 1750–1122 B.C.
Huang He Valley
Modern China
• City

ASIA
Tian Shan
TAKLIMAKAN DESERT
Kunlun Shan
MONGOLIA
(Yellow River)
Huang He
Korean Peninsula
Wei He
•Anyang
Yellow Sea
JAPAN
HIMALAYA
Plateau of Tibet
CHINA
(Yangtze River)
Chang Jiang
East China Sea
Xi Jiang
Taiwan
PACIFIC OCEAN
South China Sea
Hainan

Map Skill

REGION **Which rivers were in the Shang Empire?**

Shang Religion and Culture

The Shang believed in many gods. They made offerings to the gods to try to guarantee good harvests and victories in war. Shang kings needed to show that they had the support of the gods. If things went well in the kingdom, the people believed the gods supported the ruler. The Chinese also made offerings to the spirits of their ancestors, asking for good luck or help in time of need.

People in Shang China believed that special priests, called **oracles**, could tell the future using animal bones. A king would ask an oracle a question. The priest would carve the question onto a bone and heat it until it cracked. The priest found the answer to the question by reading the pattern of cracks on the bone.

We have learned a lot about Shang life by studying oracle bones found in Anyang. Oracle bones carry some of the earliest examples of Chinese writing. Like Egyptian hieroglyphics, Shang writing used simple pictures, or **pictographs**, to stand for objects and ideas.

A Woman General

Archaeologists working in Anyang have found more treasure in one royal tomb than in any other. This was the tomb of Fu Hao, a military leader and the wife of a Shang king. Written records found on bones and stones in her tomb describe her as a general who led 13,000 troops into battle. She also ruled her own city. Her tomb contained fine artwork and hundreds of bronze weapons and bells.

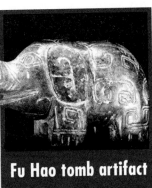

PLACES

Unlike many other Shang tombs, robbers never touched **the burial site of Fu Hao**, who may have been China's first female general. She was buried with fine ivory and jade artwork, as well as with 15 other people and 6 dogs.

Fu Hao tomb artifact

The Rise of the Zhou

After about 700 years of rule by the Shang, a nobleman named Wu Wang thought it was time for a change. Wu thought Shang rulers had become too wealthy. Around 1045 B.C., he led a rebellion that toppled the dynasty. Wu then began a dynasty of his own. The dynasty was named for his western home state, Zhou.

The Zhou would rule China for 800 years, longer than any other dynasty in Chinese history. During the Zhou rule, the Chinese developed better irrigation and flood-control systems and began using iron to make stronger plows. Zhou soldiers, using iron weapons and a new invention, the crossbow, conquered new territory and expanded the kingdom.

The Zhou also built many new roads, which helped them trade with groups farther away from the valley. Archaeologists have found silk goods from Zhou China as far away as Greece.

QUICK CHECK

Summarize How were Shang religion and government connected?

▲ An oracle bone

THE WAR FOR CHINA

By the end of the Zhou period, China's population had grown to almost 50 million. The philosopher Confucius was born during the Zhou period. His ideas would one day change Chinese society. Before that time, the region would suffer a time of brutal warfare.

The Warring States

By 403 B.C., the Zhou kings had lost much of their power, and the kingdom had split into many different states. These states waged constant war with each other to expand their power. This time in Chinese history is known as the "Period of the Warring States," and it lasted about 200 years.

During this time, many Chinese people became soldiers, because nobles ordered peasant farmers into their armies. The invention of stirrups and saddles made horses more useful in battle. Soldiers now used iron weapons, which were stronger than bronze. Fighting became brutal, and invading armies could wipe out whole villages.

A New Emperor

A young king from the state of Qin ended the Period of the Warring States in about 221 B.C. His troops took control of the Huang He delta and then conquered the northern Chinese states. The geography of the state of Qin helped bring about the prince's victory. It is protected by the Qinling Mountains on the south and the Huang He on the north, making it difficult for enemies to attack it.

The king declared himself emperor and took the name Qin Shihuangdi, or "First Grand Emperor of Qin." Eventually, the entire empire would get its name, "China," from the word Qin. Qin Shihuangdi's victory brought more of China under one leader's rule than ever before.

The emperor punished or killed anyone who opposed him. He ordered many nobles and officials to move to his capital, Xianyang, and give up their weapons. He wanted to make it difficult for them to rebel against him.

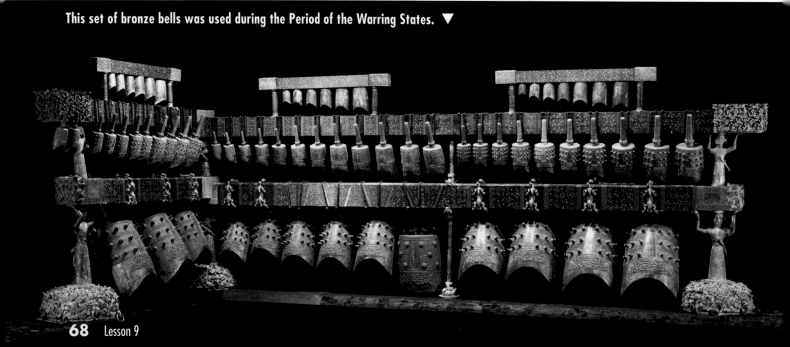

This set of bronze bells was used during the Period of the Warring States. ▼

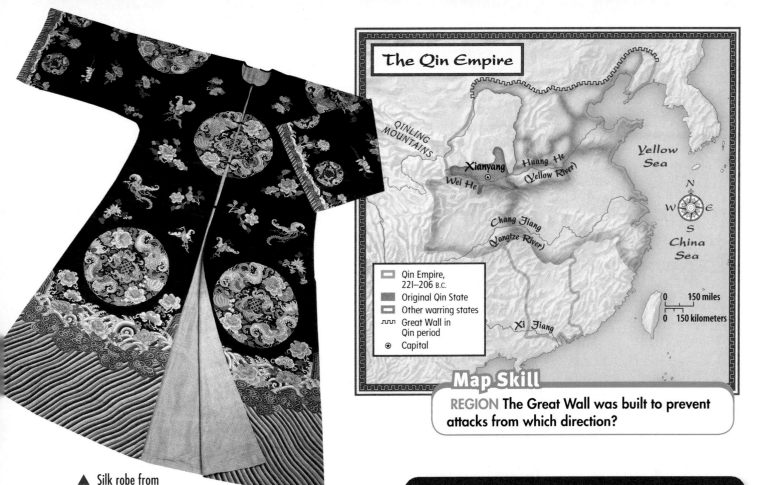

The Qin Empire

Map Skill

REGION The Great Wall was built to prevent attacks from which direction?

▲ Silk robe from the Zhou period

A Great Wall

Qin Shihuangdi often ordered farmers to leave their lands and work for him. They built roads and canals, served as soldiers, and worked on massive building projects, including a great defensive wall.

For many years, raiders on horseback had attacked villages near China's northern border. Earlier Chinese leaders had built walls for protection, and Qin Shihuangdi's workers strengthened, expanded, and linked these into a "great wall." Hundreds of years later, today's Great Wall of China would be built in the same area.

QUICK CHECK

Cause and Effect How did the Period of the Warring States change Chinese society?

Check Understanding

1. VOCABULARY Use the following words in a paragraph about daily life in Shang China.

warlord	oracle	pictograph

2. READING SKILL Cause and Effect Use your chart from page 64 to show the causes and effects of using iron weapons.

Cause	→	Effect
	→	
	→	
	→	

 3. Write About It How did the Huang He affect Chinese civilization during the first dynasties?

Lesson 10

VOCABULARY

standardization p. 71

civil service p. 74

Silk Road p. 75

READING SKILL

Cause and Effect
How did Silk Road trade change China?

Cause	→	Effect
	→	
	→	
	→	

New York Academic Content Standards
2.1, 2.2, 2.3, 3.1, 3.2

The Chinese EMPIRE

These statues of warriors guard the tomb of China's first emperor.

Visual Preview

How did early dynasties influence China?

A Qin Shihuangdi created a strong central government.

B Three major schools of thought formed between 500 and 200 B.C.

C The Han dynasty expanded the Chinese Empire.

D The Chinese made major scientific discoveries.

A THE QIN EMPIRE

Row after row, more than 7,000 armed warriors stood at attention. Each was made of clay. Farmers in northern China discovered this army of life-size statues while digging a well in 1974. The army turned out to be just a part of the incredible tomb of China's first emperor.

Around 221 B.C., Qin Shihuangdi declared that his dynasty would rule for 10,000 generations. Instead, it lasted just 15 years. Still, even in this short time, he brought major changes to China.

The emperor divided China into 36 provinces and created a central government to rule them all. Qin Shihuangdi also demanded **standardization**, the process of making things similar. For example, he ordered everyone to use the same money. He standardized the written Chinese language so that people who spoke Chinese differently could still communicate through writing.

A Massive Tomb

Qin Shihuangdi feared death. He even searched for a potion to help him live forever. His massive tomb made history. The job of building it, which began before he became emperor, took 36 years. More than 700,000 workers helped to build the emperor's tomb.

The tomb, which covers about four square miles, was found near the southern curve of the Huang He.

Archaeologists have dug at the site for more than 30 years, but they still have not reached the emperor's burial site.

The clay soldiers that guard the tomb are dressed in uniforms, and each one is individual. Clay horses, wooden chariots, and 7,000 bronze weapons are also in the tomb. This massive army was meant to protect the emperor in his death.

QUICK CHECK

Cause and Effect What was the effect of Qin Shihuangdi's standardization?

Qin Shihuangdi ▶

A WAR OF IDEAS

During the violent Period of the Warring States, Chinese thinkers developed three major schools of thought about how society should be run. Although Qin Shihuangdi backed one school of thought, the other two have had a more lasting influence on China.

The Teachings of Confucius

Confucius lived from 551 B.C. to 479 B.C. He was born to a poor family in northeastern China, and his father died when he was a boy. As a young man, he loved learning and mastered writing, mathematics, history, and even archery. He worked briefly for the government, but spent most of his life teaching.

Confucius lived during a time of great conflict, but he was sure there was a way for people to live together in peace. This idea is often summed up in what many people call Confucius's "Golden Rule":

"What you do not want done to yourself, do not do to others."

—CONFUCIUS

Confucius's teachings, or Confucianism, were collected by his students in a book called the *Analects*. Confucianism has had a tremendous impact on Chinese civilization. Confucius offered a system of moral conduct

▲ According to a Chinese legend, Laozi rode a water buffalo to the west after writing the *Dao De Jing* and was never seen again.

based on older Chinese ideas. "When you have faults, do not fear to abandon them," he said.

Confucius also believed it was important for people to respect their parents—and their ruler. A ruler also had a responsibility to be wise and good:

❝When a prince's personal conduct is correct, his government is effective without the issuing of orders.❞

Confucius believed that all men needed to be educated. Education would inspire people toward benevolence, or a tendency to do good. Anyone with the proper education and skills, and not just wealthy nobles, should be able to have a role in government, Confucius thought. He was sure that a government led by educated people would take better care of China than uneducated rulers could.

Following the Way

Another philosophy that began during this period, Daoism, also offered people a way to live peacefully. Daoists believed in the Dao, or way, a force that guided all things. They also believed people could find inner peace if they gave up their worldly desires to live a simple, moral life in harmony with nature and the Dao.

Daoist ideas are said to be based on the teachings of a philosopher named Laozi, or "the Old Master." Scholars believe Laozi lived around the same time as Confucius, but they also believe that Daoism is based on the ideas of more than one thinker. Those ideas are collected in a book called the *Dao De Jing*, or "Book of the Way." The book states:

> **"**The Dao is like a well: used but never used up. . . . It is hidden but always present. I don't know who gave birth to it.**"**

Although there are important differences between Daoism and Confucianism, many Chinese followed both schools of thought.

The School of the Law

A third group of thinkers developed a very different set of ideas about how to run China. They were led by a scholar named Han Fei, and their philosophy was called Legalism, or the School of the Law. Legalism did not promote peace. Instead, its followers believed that people were naturally evil and selfish. The Chinese needed to be controlled by a strong military and a government that would set harsh

▲ During the reign of Qin Shihuangdi, the government executed scholars and burned their books.

laws with strict punishments to force people to follow their orders.

Chinese nobles liked Legalism because it supported force and power. Qin Shihuangdi's government was based on Legalism. No one could question the ruler's authority. Anyone who opposed the emperor could be killed. Qin Shihuangdi ordered people to burn books that supported Confucianism and Daoism—and he had scholars from these schools killed.

QUICK CHECK

Cause and Effect What happened to the study of Confucianism and Daoism under Qin Shihuangdi?

C THE HAN EMPIRE

After Qin Shihuangdi's death in 210 B.C., his empire fell apart. A king named Liu Bang led the revolt against what was left of Qin's empire. He then replaced it with his own empire, the Han, in 202 B.C. Liu Bang became Han Gaozu, or "Exalted Emperor of Han."

Han Gaozu kept many practices of the Qin government, but made them less harsh. The new emperor is believed to have said that a ruler "can conquer the realm on horseback, but must dismount to rule." Still, Han armies expanded the empire into present-day North Korea, South Korea, and Vietnam, and Han emperors would rule for more than 400 years.

The Grand School

One of the strongest Han emperors was Han Wudi, who ruled from about 140 to 87 B.C. Wudi and the emperors who followed him were among the first Chinese rulers to follow some of Confucius's ideas about government.

Previous rulers had given government jobs to wealthy nobles, whether or not they were qualified. Wudi, however, set up schools where Confucian teachers prepared students for government service.

The Han Empire's most important school was called the Grand School. During Wudi's reign, only about 50 students studied there at a time. By A.D. 200, though, it had more than 30,000 students. They spent a year studying Chinese history, ethics, poetry, and folk songs, as well as Confucius's teachings. Then they took a lengthy **civil service** test. Civil service is work for the government. The test was very difficult, and most students did not pass.

The civil service system helped the government hire people based on ability rather than social position. Wealthy families still had an advantage, though, because they could more easily afford to send their sons to the Grand School. The civil service exam would remain part of Chinese culture for almost 2,000 years.

The Silk Road

By A.D. 1, when China's rulers took their first-ever national census, or population count, there were almost 60 million people in the empire. This made it the largest empire in the world. As always, most Chinese were farmers. But under the Han, more and more Chinese became involved in trade. They shipped silk and other goods to the west, southeast, and southwest.

▼ Han scholars translated ancient Chinese texts.

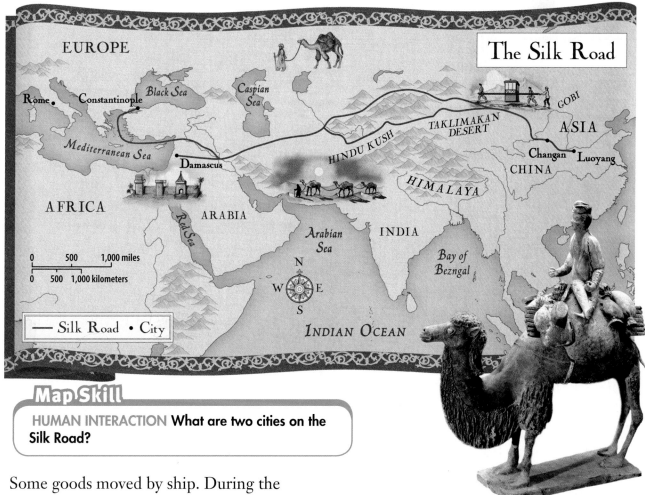

The Silk Road

EUROPE

Rome • Constantinople
Black Sea
Caspian Sea
Mediterranean Sea
Damascus
AFRICA
ARABIA
Red Sea
Arabian Sea
INDIA
Bay of Bezngal

HINDU KUSH
TAKLIMAKAN DESERT
HIMALAYA
GOBI
ASIA
Changan • Luoyang
CHINA

INDIAN OCEAN

0   500   1,000 miles
0   500   1,000 kilometers

N W E S

— Silk Road • City

Map Skill

HUMAN INTERACTION **What are two cities on the Silk Road?**

Some goods moved by ship. During the Han period, the Chinese invented the boat rudder, which helped sailors steer ships more easily. They also improved sails so ships could sail more easily into the wind. Most trade, however, went by land, along the 4,000-mile network of routes from China to the Mediterranean Sea known as the **Silk Road.** Chinese traders began using the routes around 138 B.C. The Silk Road made it possible for Chinese traders to do business with people as far away as the Roman Empire.

Traveling along the Silk Road was difficult. It crossed through wide deserts, over high mountains, and past dangerous bandits. Traders traveled in groups, with packs of camels, to make the journey safer. Trading was expensive, however, because traders had to pay taxes to each kingdom they passed through. To make money, most traders carried

▲ Traders rode camels across the Silk Road.

only expensive goods to the west, such as silk, porcelain, tea, and spices.

Buddhism Reaches China

As Chinese traders traveled back and forth along the Silk Road, they learned about other cultures and their ideas. Around 125 B.C., some Chinese officials returned from India with information about the Buddhist religion. Over the next few centuries, merchants and teachers from India introduced Buddhism to many Chinese people. The religion gained many followers in China after the fall of the Han.

QUICK CHECK

Cause and Effect How did Confucius's ideas influence the Han dynasty?

75

Chinese scientists, artists, and inventors made great advances during the Han Empire. Like the ancient Egyptians, the Chinese learned to predict eclipses of the sun. Medicine improved as doctors discovered ways, such as using certain herbs, to treat illness. Some of these methods are still used today by those practicing traditional Chinese medicine.

Writers thrived under the Han as well, and the Chinese written language grew from 3,000 to 9,000 characters. In A.D. 100, scholars created the first Chinese dictionary. Writers wrote their ideas on the paper invented by craftworkers. Han paper was similar to the papyrus created by ancient Egyptians. The Chinese made a watery mixture of mulberry tree fibers and then drained off the water. Government officials also used paper to keep track of the population and tax payments.

Steel was also invented during the Han period, as scientists learned to combine iron and carbon. Steel was stronger than many other metals in use at the time. Other new tools made life easier as well. Waterwheels could grind more grain, and iron drill bits helped people dig better wells so they could draw saltwater and mine salt from it.

Predicting Earthquakes

One of the most amazing Han inventions was the seismograph, a device that could predict and locate earthquakes. This seismograph looked like a bronze vase with eight dragon heads on it. Each dragon held a ball in its mouth. When the ground shook, a tube that hung inside the vase would vibrate, causing the ball to fall out of one dragon's mouth and into the mouth of a bronze toad sitting under it. This told the government in which direction the earthquake had occurred so that help could be sent quickly.

Citizenship

Disaster Relief

One responsibility of government is to help citizens when natural disasters strike. Because of its location, China often suffers earthquakes, floods, and forest fires. Just as Han emperors used seismographs to figure out where to send help when earthquakes hit, Chinese leaders today use satellite technology to decide how best to help communities hit by disaster. Individual citizens help each other in times of need as well. When Hurricane Katrina struck Louisiana and Mississippi in 2005, Americans donated more than $4 billion to support their neighbors.

Write About It How can people in your community help victims of a natural disaster?

Vibrations from an earthquake shook the seismograph, causing a ball to fall into a frog's mouth. ▶

The Han Legacy

Like every dynasty that came before it, the Han eventually fell. Failed military campaigns on the outer edges of the empire, quarrels among local leaders, and a series of weak emperors caused the collapse. In A.D. 190, rebel armies attacked the capital city of Luoyang, and, by 220, the dynasty had fallen. During the violent fighting among local rulers that followed the fall of the Han, many more Chinese turned to Buddhism.

The Han dynasty had proved that Chinese rulers could follow Confucian ideas about education, fairness, and behavior and still lead a mighty empire. The dynasty is considered so important in the development of Chinese government and culture that, even today, a large group of ethnic Chinese people still call themselves "the Han."

QUICK CHECK

Summarize **How did China change during the Han dynasty?**

Check Understanding

1. **VOCABULARY** Use the vocabulary words to write a paragraph about life in Han China.

   standardization   Silk Road
   civil service

2. **READING SKILL Cause and Effect** Use your chart on page 70 to explain how Silk Road trade changed China.

Cause	→	Effect
	→	
	→	
	→	

 EXPLORE The Big Idea **3. Write About It** How did the Han Empire change as it grew larger?

Vocabulary

Write a sentence or more to answer each question.

1. Why are Old Stone Age tools considered the first technology?

2. How did Babylon become an important city-state in Mesopotamia?

3. How do people pay for products in a barter society?

4. How do the monsoon winds affect India's climate?

Comprehension and Critical Thinking

5. How did hunter-gatherers get food?

6. How do artifacts at Harappa help archaeologists reconstruct the life of its people?

7. **Reading Skill** What caused Asoka to stop fighting wars?

8. **Critical Thinking** How do oral traditions help preserve a culture?

9. **Critical Thinking** Why did many ancient cultures begin along large rivers?

Skill

Use Topographic Maps

Write a complete sentence to answer each question.

10. Where is the highest land in South Korea?

11. What is the elevation of western North Korea?

12. How can a topographical map help you to understand how a civilization grows?

Topographic Map of Korean Peninsula

CHINA

Paektu San
9,100 feet

1,000'

1,000'

2,000'

5,000'

2,000'

NORTH
KOREA

Sea of
Japan

Yellow
Sea

1,000'

SOUTH
KOREA

N
W E
S

0   100   200 miles
0 100   200 kilometers

Elevation (feet)
5,000–9,999
2,000–4,999
1,000–1,999
0–999
▲ Mountain peak

New York English Language Arts Test Preparation

Directions

Read this passage about Ramses II. Then answer questions 1 and 2.

Ramses II ordered more monuments built than any other pharaoh. The Temple of Abu Simbel is one of the most astonishing monuments ever created. Four gigantic statues of Ramses II guard the entrance. He also ordered the building of monuments to celebrate his victories.

Some scholars think that Ramses II is the pharaoh in the Book of Exodus in the Hebrew Bible. He is also the subject of a poem by the English poet Percy Shelley. Ramses II is probably the most famous of all Egyptian pharaohs.

---

1 What is the main idea of this passage?

- **A** Egyptian history
- **B** the Legend of Ramses II
- **C** the works of Percy Shelley
- **D** Egyptian Architecture

2 What did Ramses II have built to celebrate his victories?

- **A** monuments
- **B** statues
- **C** pyramids
- **D** palaces

The Big Idea Activities

How does geography affect civilizations?

Write About the Big Idea

Narrative Essay
In Unit 1, you read about how geography affected early civilizations. Use your notes in your foldable to write an essay.

Begin with an introductory paragraph, stating geography's effect on civilizations.

Write a paragraph describing how each civilization was affected by geography.

Your final paragraph should summarize the main ideas of your essay.

Mesopotamia
Egypt
India
China

Make a Brochure

Work in small groups to prepare a travel brochure for one of the civilizations you studied in Unit 1.

1. Brainstorm to select the location you will include in your brochure.

2. Some members of your group should write descriptions of what a tourist might visit.

3. Some members of your group may draw pictures of "tourist attractions."

4. You may want to photocopy your brochures so others can see them.

5. Allow time to color your brochures after they are photocopied.

THE ANCIENT WORLD

▼ The ruins of the Oracle at Delphi.

Unit 2

EXPLORE The Big Idea

Essential Question
Why do empires rise and fall?

FOLDABLES Study Organizer

Fact and Opinion
Make a concept map foldable to take notes as you read Unit 2. Your notes will help you answer the Big Idea question. Your foldable's title will be **Empires Rise and Fall**. Your foldable will have three tabs, labeled **Greece**, **Rome**, and **Americas**.

Empires Rise and Fall
Greece   Rome   Americas

LOG ON

For more about Unit 2 go to
www.macmillanmh.com

81

PEOPLE, PLACES, AND EVENTS

Homer

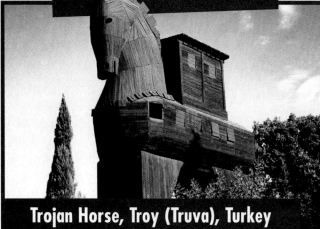

Trojan Horse, Troy (Truva), Turkey

700 B.C.
Homer creates the *Iliad* and the *Odyssey*

Augustus

Pantheon, Rome, Italy

27 B.C.
Augustus becomes first Roman emperor

1000 BC   **500 BC**   **AD 1**

The Greek poet **Homer** was blind, but he created two poems about a long-ago war between Greece and the city-state of **Troy**.

Today you can visit the ruins of Troy and see a copy of the famous Trojan Horse.

Octavian defeated all his rivals and became the first emperor of **Rome**. He changed his name to **Augustus** and built the Roman Empire.

Today you can see ruins of many famous Roman buildings in Italy and across Europe.

LOG ON

For more about People, Places, and Events, visit:
www.macmillanmh.com

Theodora

Hagia Sophia, Istanbul, Turkey

A.D.537

Justinian and
Theodora rule
Byzantine Empire

Pachakuti

Machu Picchu, Peru

A.D.1450

Pachakuti builds
Machu Picchu

AD 500   AD 1000   AD 1500

Empress Theodora married the Byzantine emperor Justinian and ruled from their capital of **Constantinople** (Istanbul, Turkey).

Today you can go to Istanbul and see Hagia Sophia, the cathedral built by Justinian.

Pachakuti united a large empire in the Andes Mountains of South America.

Today you can visit **Machu Picchu**, a group of palaces built by Pachakuti high in the Andes Mountains of Peru.

GREEK CIVILIZATION

A temple porch in Athens, Greece

Visual Preview

How did earlier civilizations shape Greek culture?

A Ancient Greeks depended on the sea for food and trade.

B Three earlier Mediterranean civilizations influenced the culture of Greece.

C Greek gods were believed to control many natural events.

84

GREECE'S GEOGRAPHY

The ship was loaded with goods. It had been a difficult journey—twice they had been blown off course. Now, they could see coastline spotted with green olive trees. The sailors cheered—they were home at last!

Greece is a mountainous land on the European coast of the Mediterranean Sea. Over 400 islands lie off the coast, while two peninsulas make up mainland Greece. Attica, a small, triangular-shaped peninsula, has many **harbors**. Harbors are sheltered places along the coast. To the south is a peninsula called the Peloponnesus. Mountains and seas divide areas from one another. As a result, early Greek cities communities grew up fiercely independent.

Farming

Much of Greece is covered with mountains and rocky soil, mostly unsuitable for farming. Greek farmers met the challenges of rocky soil by growing crops that grew well in the harsh environment. One major crop was olives, which were a staple of Greek life. They were served as food and were made into oil, which was used for cooking and fuel.

Greek farmers also raised sheep and goats. These animals ate the plants that grew on Greece's mountains. Food was scarce, however, no matter how hard the Greek farmers worked. They had to rely on the sea to survive.

The Greek Economy

Most Greeks lived within 40 miles of the sea, which helped link them to the rest of the world. They became fishers, sailors, shipbuilders, and traders. Greek merchants, with their sturdy boats and sailing knowledge, bought grain from surrounding areas. These traders traveled as far as Egypt and Spain to conduct business.

QUICK CHECK

Fact and Opinion Write one fact and one opinion about the geography of Greece.

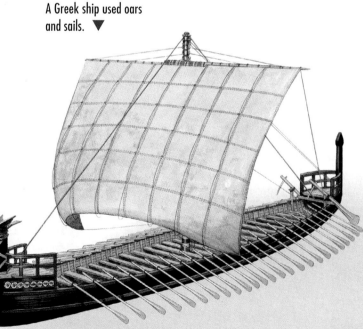

A Greek ship used oars and sails. ▼

B TRADING CIVILIZATIONS

Three early trading civilizations sailed the Mediterranean Sea. The Minoans, the Mycenaeans, and the Phoenicians helped create the ancient Greek culture.

The Minoans

The Minoans lived on the island of Crete. They were expert traders who took their goods across the Mediterranean Sea. They grew so wealthy from trade that their ruler's palace at Knossos had more than 1,000 rooms! By 2000 B.C., the Minoans controlled the trade of the eastern Mediterranean. Some historians believe that a **tsunami**, or tidal wave, may have washed over Crete around 1450 B.C. This may have allowed the Mycenaean Greeks to conquer the weakened Minoans.

The Mycenaeans

The Mycenaeans came to Greece from central Asia in about 1900 B.C. They captured the Greek mainland and established small kingdoms. Each kingdom was centered around a protected palace on a hill. These hilltop forts

Below are the ruins at Knossos. The drawing shows what they might have looked like.

ARTIFACTS FROM ANCIENT GREECE

◄ A golden burial mask from Mycenae

◄ Minoan bull

▲ Phoenician glass perfume bottle

were centers of trade in peace and provided protection during war.

Earthquakes and wars between the kingdoms weakened Mycenaean civilization. Around 1200 B.C., the Mycenaeans were conquered by invaders called Dorians. The Dorians made iron weapons, a great advantage against the Mycenaeans, who had only bronze—a softer metal. By about 1150 B.C., Mycenaean civilization had collapsed.

The Phoenicians

Phoenicia was a land in the eastern Mediterranean, in what is today Lebanon. Like the Greeks, Phoenicians looked to the sea for survival. Beginning as early as 3000 B.C. they sailed across the Mediterranean as traders. Along their routes, they established colonies. A colony is an area under the control of another, usually distant, country.

Phoenician city-states produced trade goods such as cloth, engraved metals, and glass objects. The city-states of Sidon and Tyre were especially famous for a purple dye made from a certain kind of seashell. This purple dye was one of the most valuable trade goods in the Mediterranean world for the next 2,500 years.

A Phoenician Invention

Phoenicians spread culture and ideas along with their trade goods. This cultural diffusion created new ideas and better products. The greatest Phoenician invention was their alphabet. This alphabet is the basis for the alphabet we use today. In fact, our letters B, L, and O were first used by Phoenician traders.

The ancient Greeks adapted the Phoenician alphabet to write their own language. It made reading and writing Greek much simpler. Soon people were writing down tales that had been passed down orally by storytellers for many generations.

QUICK CHECK

Fact and Opinion Using facts from this lesson, write an opinion about the Phoenicians.

GREEK RELIGION AND CULTURE

The Greeks practiced polytheism. According to Greek mythology, there were 12 main gods and goddesses who lived on Mount Olympus, Greece's highest mountain. The ancient Greeks believed that their gods and goddesses played roles in daily life.

They also believed their gods controlled natural events, such as earthquakes and storms. Many festivals honored the Greek gods. For example, the Olympic Games honored Zeus. These games were so important that wars were halted while the games were played.

GODS AND GODDESSES OF GREECE

Poseidon, god of the sea and storms

Aphrodite, goddess of love and beauty

Hephaistos, god of metalworking

Ares, god of battle

Hades, god of the Underworld and wealth

Athena, goddess of wisdom and peace

Artemis, goddess of the moon and of hunting

Demeter, goddess of agriculture

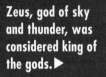

Zeus, god of sky and thunder, was considered king of the gods. ▶

Hera, Zeus's wife, the goddess of marriage

Apollo, god of the sun, music, and medicine

Hestia, goddess of fire and the home

Philosophy

Greek **philosophers** studied history, political science, science, and mathematics. A philosopher is a "lover of wisdom." Besides being great thinkers, Greek philosophers often taught students, as well.

In the mid-400s B.C., a philosopher named Socrates led discussions about ways to live. Socrates angered some people in his city, Athens, because he began to question the city's laws, customs, and even religion. In 399 B.C., Socrates was brought to trial for "urging Athens' young people to revolt." He was sentenced to death. His student, Plato, wrote down Socrates' ideas. Plato later became a teacher with his own famous student named Aristotle.

Greek Drama and Epics

Greek plays included comedies and dramas, and they were presented in outdoor theaters. A comedy is a play that ends happily, and in a tragedy, the main character is defeated or dies. Actors wore masks. Frowning masks represented tragic figures, and smiling masks represented characters in comedy. These masks are still used today as symbols of acting and theater.

The Greeks enjoyed poems that described Greek history. One of the most famous ancient Greek poets was Homer. He created two epics, or long poems that tell the story of legendary figures. In the *Iliad*, Homer described a war between the Greeks and Trojans. In the *Odyssey* he described the adventures of the hero, Odysseus, who left the Greek army at the end of the Trojan war and took nearly 20 years to return home!

▲ Greek actor wearing a comic mask.

QUICK CHECK

Fact and Opinion Based on the reaction of Athens, do you think Socrates' statements were facts or opinions?

Check Understanding

1. **VOCABULARY** Write a paragraph about life in ancient Greece using these vocabulary words.

    harbor   **tsunami**   **philosopher**

2. **READING SKILL Fact and Opinion** Use your completed chart from page 84 to write a paragraph about the ancient Greek economy.

Fact	Opinion

3. **Write About It** Write about how the geography of ancient Greece contributed to the rise of civilization in that region.

89

Lesson 2

VOCABULARY

monarchy p. 91

tyrant p. 91

oligarchy p. 91

democracy p. 91

plague p. 93

READING SKILL

Fact and Opinion
Use this chart to list facts and then your opinions about Athens and Sparta.

Fact	Opinion

New York Academic Content Standards

2.1, 2.2, 2.3, 3.1, 3.2

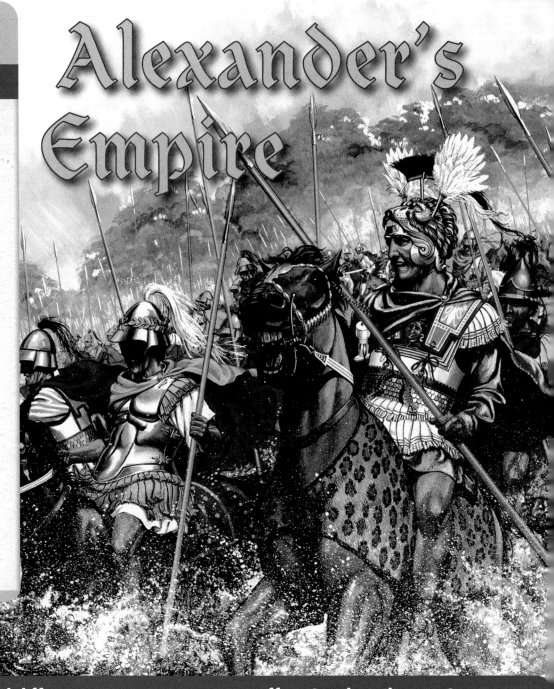

Alexander's Empire

Alexander leads his troops into battle with the Persians.

Visual Preview

How did different government systems affect Greek civilization?

A Greek city-states had a variety of governments and did not unite politically.

B Greek city-states were weakened by wars with Persia and among themselves.

C Alexander was a brilliant general and the leader of the Greek-influenced world.

Ⓐ THE GROWTH OF CITY-STATES

By 700 B.C., Greek culture had spread around the Aegean Sea. The small city-states remained independent of each other. Each region had one city at its heart. The Greek word for this kind of city-state was polis.

Most city-states were built around an acropolis, a walled hill where people could seek safety from attack. Near the acropolis was an agora, a market and meeting area.

Governing City-States

Some city-states were ruled by one person. A **monarchy** was ruled by a king. If one person took control of a city state by force, that person was known as a **tyrant**. Today, we call a cruel and unfair ruler a tyrant.

Other city states were ruled by groups. An **oligarchy** was a government of the wealthy and powerful. A few cities had a **democracy**, where all citizens participated. Only men could be citizens. Greek democracy influenced many later nations, including the United States.

QUICK CHECK

Fact and Opinion In your opinion, which kind of government is best for a city-state?

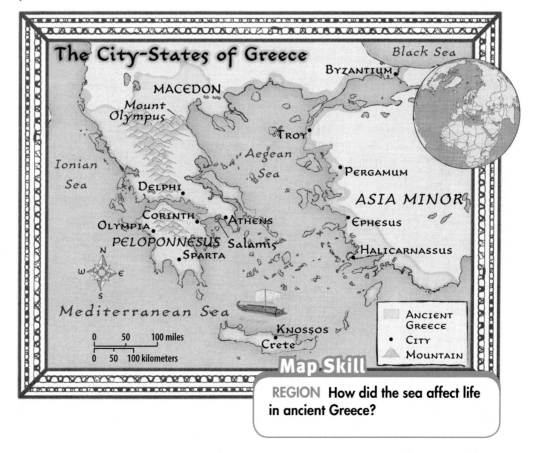

Map Skill

REGION How did the sea affect life in ancient Greece?

91

EMPIRES IN THE MEDITERRANEAN

By about 500 B.C., the two most powerful city-states in Greece were Athens and Sparta. They had different values and cultures, and they often fought with each other and with other city-states.

War With Persia

The Persians came from what is now Iran. In 539 B.C., Persian armies conquered Greek city-states along the coast of Asia Minor in what is today called Turkey.

The Persian king Darius attacked Greece in 490 B.C. To his surprise, his powerful forces were defeated on both land and sea by much smaller Greek armies and navies. Afterwards, Persia remained an enemy of Greece.

SPARTA VERSUS ATHENS

SPARTA		ATHENS
• Two kings • Council of elders	GOVERNMENT	• Limited democracy • All citizens voted • Only males were citizens
• Boys trained for military • Girls trained to be mothers of soldiers	EDUCATION	• Wealthy boys went to school • Poor boys learned a trade • Girls were taught at home
• Women had some legal rights	WOMEN	• Women had few rights and rarely appeared in public

The Peloponnesian War

After the war with Persia, Athens became rich and powerful. Other city-states grew jealous and afraid of Athens. In 431 B.C., Sparta and its allies attacked Athens, beginning the Peloponnesian War.

The Athenians hid behind their walls and used their navy to bring food into the city. As the war continued, a **plague** broke out in Athens, killing a third of the city. A plague is a disease or event that causes suffering for many people. Among the dead was their ruler, Pericles. Weakened by plague and lacking a strong leader, the city surrendered in 404 B.C. The victory did Sparta little good. Greece was exhausted by war, and a new empire was rising in the north.

QUICK CHECK

Fact and Opinion Is Thucydides stating a fact or an opinion in the Datagraphic on the right? Explain your answer.

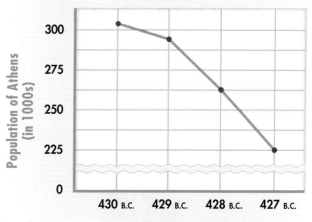

DataGraphic

Plague in Athens, 430 B.C.

In the Peloponnesian War, people crowded into Athens for safety. Then a deadly plague swept through the city. One Athenian wrote:

❝The bodies of dying men lay one upon another. The half-dead moved about the streets. The places in which they stayed were full of corpses.❞

—THUCYDIDES

The Plague in Athens

Population of Athens (in 1000s) vs. Years of the Plague in Athens

| 430 B.C. | 429 B.C. | 428 B.C. | 427 B.C. |

Think About It How does the information in the line graph support the words of Thucydides?

▲ The Acropolis in Athens is now a ruin.

C   A NEW POWER

Macedonia was a country north of Greece. Its army used soldiers on horseback, or cavalry, which proved more effective than soldiers on foot. By 338 B.C., their king, Philip, had conquered all the city-states of the Greek mainland. Philip was murdered in 336 B.C., leaving his 20-year-old son, Alexander, ruler of the Greek world.

Alexander the Great

From the age of 16, Alexander was trained to be a general. In 334 B.C., he led his army on a war of conquest against Persia. First he conquered Asia Minor and Egypt. Then, he continued east into Persia. After a three–year war, he defeated the powerful Persian army and captured their treasury. The Greeks' ancient enemy had been subdued.

Eager for more conquests, Alexander continued east. His soldiers invaded India

and defeated local rulers. At the age of 32, Alexander was the ruler of the largest empire in the world. He made ancient Babylon his capital, where he died suddenly in 323 B.C.

After Alexander's death, his empire was divided by his generals. His death began a period called the Hellenistic era. The word Hellenistic means "like the Greeks." Greek language, customs, and culture spread around the Mediterranean world and influenced life in the region for the next 700 years.

QUICK CHECK

Fact and Opinion Is it a fact or an opinion that Alexander was "the Great"? Use examples from the text to support your answer.

Alexander the Great defeating an enemy in battle ▶

Check Understanding

1. **VOCABULARY** Use the following vocabulary words to write a summary of government in ancient Greece.

   tyrant   oligarchy   democracy

2. **READING SKILL Fact and Opinion** Use the chart from page 90 to write two facts and two opinions about the culture of Athens and of Sparta.

Fact	Opinion

3. **Write About It** Write a paragraph about the rise and fall of Alexander's empire.

Map and Globe Skills

Use Historical Maps

VOCABULARY

historical map

A **historical map** shows places and events in the past. For example, the map on this page shows the empire of Alexander in 332 B.C. It shows cities and boundaries that existed at that time. To read historical maps, follow the steps below.

Learn It

- Read the map title. It identifies the places and time period of the map.

- Look at the map legend. It identifies colors and symbols on the historical map.

Try It

- What is the title of the map on this page?

- In what year was the battle of Issus?

- How many miles wide was Alexander's empire from east to west?

Apply It

- Compare this historical map to a modern map of the same region. How are the maps similar and different?

- What would you include in a historical map of your community?

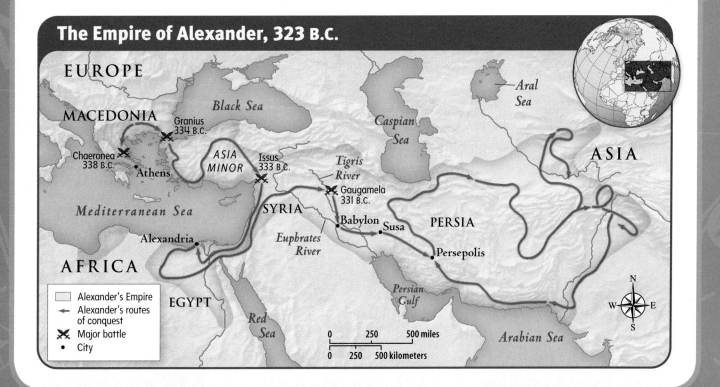

The Empire of Alexander, 323 B.C.

EUROPE
MACEDONIA
Granius 334 B.C.
Black Sea
Caspian Sea
Aral Sea
ASIA
Chaeronea 338 B.C.
Athens
ASIA MINOR
Issus 333 B.C.
Tigris River
Gaugamela 331 B.C.
Mediterranean Sea
SYRIA
Babylon Susa
PERSIA
Alexandria
Euphrates River
Persepolis
AFRICA
EGYPT
Persian Gulf
Red Sea
Arabian Sea

Legend:
- Alexander's Empire
- Alexander's routes of conquest
- Major battle
- City

0   250   500 miles
0   250   500 kilometers

Lesson 3

VOCABULARY

republic p. 98

patrician p. 98

plebeian p. 98

consul p. 98

civil war p. 100

READING SKILL

Fact and Opinion
Fill out the chart with facts and opinions about the rights of plebeians in ancient Rome.

Facts	Opinions

New York Academic Content Standards
2.1, 2.2, 2.3, 3.1, 3.2, 5.1

THE ROMAN REPUBLIC

Fields in northern Italy

Visual Preview

How did Roman society shape the Republic?

A The city of Rome was founded on seven hills.

B Rome had a republic, a government with elected leaders.

C Winning the Punic Wars gave Rome control of the Mediterranean region.

96

A ITALY'S GEOGRAPHY

Legend says that Rome was founded in 753 B.C. by brothers called Romulus and Remus. Rome's seven hills made Rome easy to defend, and the Tiber River served as a water route to the Mediterranean Sea.

Italy's geography influenced the country's history. Mountains called the Alps form a wall to the north, separating Italy from the rest of Europe. Italy is also a peninsula. Early Italians traded with Greece, Egypt, and other neighboring cultures. As a result, early Italian culture was influenced more by cultures around the sea than cultures across the Alps.

Plains and Mountains

The Italian peninsula pokes out into the Mediterranean Sea like a boot. Looking at Italy on a map you can easily see the "heel" and the "toe" of the boot. The island to the west of the toe is called Sicily. It was a popular destination for ancient Greek colonists because of its rich farmland.

Along with the Alps, the Apennines affected life in Italy. These mountains run all the way down the boot from north to south, and their height made travel across the peninsula difficult. Italy also has volcanoes, such as Mount Etna in Sicily. Perhaps the most famous is Mount Vesuvius. Its eruption in A.D. 79 buried the crowded cities of Pompeii and Herculaneum.

Italy also has a number of fertile plains. One of the most important is in the Po River valley. Another is Latium, located on the west coast of central Italy. The Tiber River runs through the center of this plain. More than 2,000 years ago, a city located on the Tiber River was the center of a vast empire. The name of this city was Rome.

QUICK CHECK

Fact and Opinion State one fact and one opinion from this section about Italy's geography.

◀ Mount Etna

Ⓑ RULERS OF ROME

The Etruscans were among the earliest people in Italy. Early in its history, Rome was ruled by Etruscan kings. In 510 B.C., the Romans drove out these kings and founded the Roman **Republic**. In a republic, government leaders are voted into office.

Patricians and Plebians

A powerful group called **patricians**, from Rome's wealthiest families, became the new rulers. Beneath them were **plebians**, poor farmers and shopkeeprs who could not hold office. Both groups were made up of Roman citizens. A citizen is a person who is born in a country or who becomes a member of a country by law.

From its beginnings, Rome was a military power. By 250 B.C., Rome had conquered most of the Italian peninsula. The conquered people eventually became Roman citizens. Citizens of Rome paid taxes, and male citizens served in the army.

Rome had two elected leaders, called **consuls**. There were two so that neither man could take advantage and become a dictator, an oppressive ruler. Both consuls had to agree on any public plan, and either consul could veto, or turn down, a plan of the other consul. To be certain that there would be no dictator, the Senate, the lawmaking body of Rome, had to approve the consuls' plans.

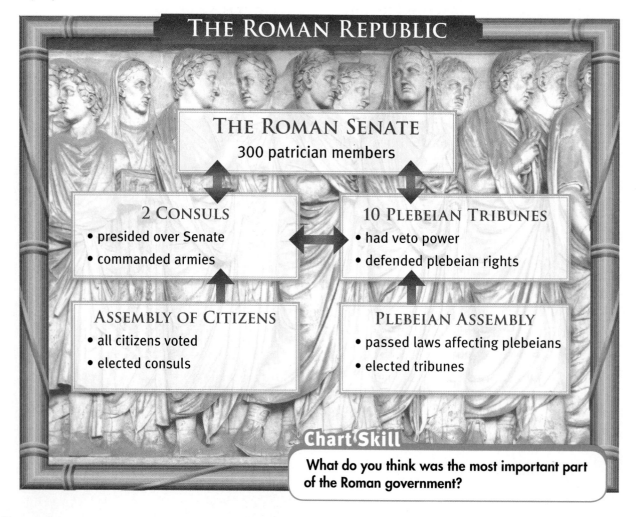

THE ROMAN REPUBLIC

THE ROMAN SENATE
300 patrician members

2 CONSULS
- presided over Senate
- commanded armies

10 PLEBEIAN TRIBUNES
- had veto power
- defended plebeian rights

ASSEMBLY OF CITIZENS
- all citizens voted
- elected consuls

PLEBEIAN ASSEMBLY
- passed laws affecting plebeians
- elected tribunes

Chart Skill

What do you think was the most important part of the Roman government?

▲ A Roman mosaic shows gladiators fighting in the arena.

Plebeian Demands

Do you think this patrician government was fair? Plebeians did not. They were citizens. They served in the army and paid taxes. Why did patricians have all the political power?

In 494 B.C., the plebeians came up with a clever plan—they went on strike! Plebeians refused to open their shops or to serve in the army. Plebeian farmers refused to bring their crops into Rome. The panicked patricians had to agree to share power. The plebeians were given a plebeian assembly to elect representatives called tribunes. The tribunes could veto laws and review judges' decisions.

About 50 years later, plebeians had a new demand. They said they had no idea what the laws were because they were not posted. All Roman laws were then placed on display in Rome's public marketplace. The laws were referred to as the Twelve Tables because they were carved on twelve large stone tablets.

A Slave Revolt

There was a third group of people living in Rome. Hundreds of enslaved people were captured during wars. Anyone of any race could be enslaved. Roman slaves had some legal rights—they could even buy their freedom. Life, however, was usually harsh for slaves. It was especially so for a group of slaves called gladiators.

Gladiators fought each other or wild animals to the death in large arenas. It was a dangerous life. In 73 B.C., 70,000 slaves joined a gladiator named Spartacus in revolt. His army of slaves swept across the peninsula. In the end, Spartacus and his followers were defeated and put to death. This ended any serious resistance to slavery in the Roman world.

QUICK CHECK

Fact and Opinion In your opinion, was the government of Rome fair?

99

A POWERFUL ENEMY

Carthage was a Phoenician city-state in northern Africa. For over a century, Rome and Carthage struggled for power. Historians call these the Punic Wars, from *Punicus*, the Roman word for "Phoenicia."

I came.

I saw.

I conquered.

—JULIUS CAESAR

The Punic Wars

In 218 B.C., an army from Carthage crossed the Alps and invaded Italy. Their brilliant general, Hannibal, delivered a crushing defeat to Rome. Rome then invaded northern Africa, and Hannibal had to return to defend Carthage.

Both cities knew it was a battle to the death. The Romans finally defeated Carthage in 146 B.C. They sold the survivors into slavery and burned every building in Carthage. Legend says they poured salt on the soil so nothing would grow there again. Rome now ruled the Mediterranean world.

A Battle for Power

After the Punic Wars ended, several **civil wars** erupted between wealthy Romans and powerful generals. A civil war is a war between groups within a country. One of these generals was Julius Caesar. In 58 B.C., his armies conquered Gaul, present-day

France. He became wildly popular and later led his soldiers into Rome. Once there, he made himself dictator for life.

Caesar made many changes. He revised the Roman calendar. He gave land and grain to the poor. He increased the number of people in the Senate and granted citizenship to foreigners. Caesar, however, had many enemies.

QUICK CHECK

Cause and Effect **What did Caesar do after leaving Gaul?**

Check Understanding

1. **VOCABULARY** Write a letter from ancient Rome. Tell about Rome's government using these vocabulary words.

   republic   **patrician**   **plebeian**   **consul**

2. **READING SKILL Identify Fact and Opinion** Use your chart from page 96 to write a letter to the Roman Senate. Tell your opinion about giving more rights to plebeians. Use facts to support your opinion.

Fact	Opinion

3. **Write About It** Write about how Italy's geography affected the rise of Rome.

Chart and Graph Skills

Use Double Bar Graph

VOCABULARY

double bar graph

A **double bar graph** compares information. It shows information as two bars on the same graph. Look at the double bar graph on this page as you follow the steps.

Learn It

- A double bar graph uses bars side by side to compare information.

- The title shows the topic of the double bar graph.

- The bars use different colors to show each set of information clearly.

- The labels on each side of the graph tell you how to understand the information.

Try It

- Which army was larger?

- Which army suffered more casualties?

Apply It

- Make a double bar graph showing the number of boys and the number of girls in each sixth-grade class in your school.

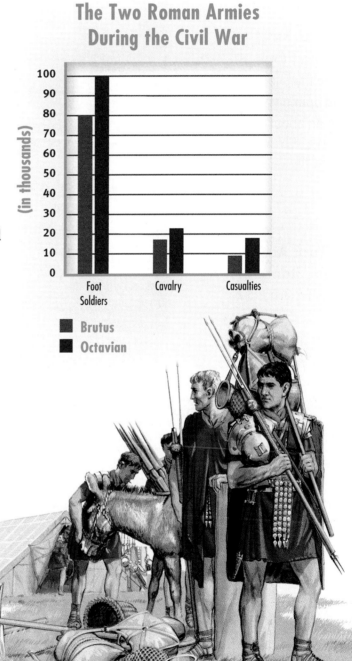

The Two Roman Armies During the Civil War

(in thousands)

100, 90, 80, 70, 60, 50, 40, 30, 20, 10, 0

Foot Soldiers — Cavalry — Casualties

■ Brutus
■ Octavian

VOCABULARY

Pax Romana p. 104

census p. 104

aqueduct p. 104

inflation p. 105

READING SKILL

Fact and Opinion
Fill in the chart with facts and opinions from the lesson about Octavian.

Fact	Opinion

New York Academic Content Standards
2.1, 2.2, 2.3, 3.1, 3.2

THE ROMAN EMPIRE

Roman senators murder Julius Caesar.

Visual Preview

How did change impact the Roman world?

A Octavian won the civil war and became emperor after Julius Caesar died.

B Augustus established the Roman Empire, which lasted until A.D. 476.

C Christianity became the religion of the Roman Empire.

D The Byzantine Empire continued Roman traditions for another 1,000 years.

A FROM REPUBLIC TO EMPIRE

Tradition says Caesar ignored a warning to "beware the Ides of March," March 15. On that date in 44 B.C., Caesar's enemies surrounded him at the Senate building and stabbed him to death.

Civil war followed Caesar's death. On one side were forces led by those who had killed Caesar. On the other side were his grandnephew Octavian and the generals Antony and Lepidus. These three men defeated Caesar's killers in 43 B.C.

Civil War Continues

Peace would not last long. Octavian soon forced Lepidus to retire. Then he and Antony divided the Roman world between themselves. Octavian took the west. Antony took the East.

Octavian and Antony soon came into conflict. Antony fell in love with the Egyptian queen, Cleopatra, and formed an alliance with her. Octavian told the Romans that Antony, with Cleopatra's help, planned to make himself the ruler of the republic. This alarmed the Senate, which then supported Octavian in a war against Antony.

Octavian crushed the army and navy of Antony and Cleopatra at the Battle of Actium in 31 B.C. The couple then fled to Egypt, where they killed themselves. Octavian now stood alone at the top of the Roman world. The period of the civil wars was over, but so was the republic.

Cleopatra ▶

Octavian Becomes Augustus

After his victory, Octavian was named *imperator*, or "one who commands." Our word *emperor* comes from *imperator*. Octavian had the power to veto any law, rule all Roman provinces, and to control the army.

As a sign of Octavian's power, the Senate gave him the name Augustus, meaning "honored one." Augustus set about reforming the government, reorganizing the empire, and creating a permanent army and navy. Our month of August is named in his honor.

QUICK CHECK

Fact and Opinion How did Octavian influence public opinion against Antony? Do you think the facts supported his opinion?

THE ROMAN PEACE

For centuries, the Mediterranean region had been filled with conflict. Under Augustus and his successors, the region was under the control of one empire. Augustus's rule began the **Pax Romana**, or "Roman Peace." This peace lasted nearly 200 years.

Augustus's Empire

Augustus rebuilt Rome with stately palaces, fountains, and splendid public buildings. The arts flourished as never before. Augustus ordered a system of roads built to connect Rome to every part of the empire. Once built, they helped to make communication, trade, and travel throughout the empire possible.

Augustus devoted much of his energy to improving Rome's government. A **census**, or count of the population, was taken. The tax code was reformed, and laws were changed to increase the power of the government. This helped to unify the vast territories of the empire.

Roman cities enjoyed police and fire protection. **Aqueducts**, long stone structures, were built to bring fresh water into cities. Many Roman cities had huge public baths with picture galleries and libraries. For entertainment, gladiator matches and chariot races were common across the empire.

THE **ROMAN EMPIRE** A.D. 130

Hadrian's Wall

Britannia (Britain)

Londinium (London)

Germania (Germany)

EUROPA (Europe)

OCEANUS ATLANTICUS (ATLANTIC OCEAN)

Gallia (France)

Pontus Euxinus (Black Sea)

Iberia (Spain)

Roma (Rome)

Italia (Italy)

Graecia (Greece)

ASIA

Actium

AFRICA

Mare Internum (Mediterranean Sea)

Alexandria

0   200   400 miles
0   200   400 kilometers

Aegyptus (Egypt)

Map Skill

MOVEMENT **How did the Mediterranean Sea affect the lands of the Roman Empire?**

▲ Enemies burn the conquered city of Rome.

The Fall of Rome

By A.D. 200, the Empire began to decline. New civil wars, combined with Germanic and Persian invasions, weakened the economy. A common problem the economy suffered was **inflation**. This was the rapid increase in prices. One effect of inflation was less income. With less income, fewer taxes were paid and the Empire could not afford to defend its borders.

To better govern the empire, the emperor Diocletian divided it into a western and eastern empire in A.D. 293. His successor, Constantine, moved the center of power to a city in the east called Byzantium. In honor of himself, he renamed the city Constantinople.

The western empire shrank in importance and power. Finally, in A.D. 476, a Germanic tribe conquered the city of Rome. Even so, the influence of Rome would outlive its empire. Roman traditions continued in the eastern, or Byzantine, empire for almost one thousand years. In the west, small Germanic kingdoms adopted Roman laws, customs, and language.

QUICK CHECK

Cause and Effect What was a long-term effect of inflation in the Roman Empire?

Citizenship

Citizenship Then and Now

Roman citizenship was a prized possession. To gain Roman citizenship, a person could serve in the army or work for the government. Some bought their citizenship, but for a very high price. Today, immigrants to the United States must pass a test and promise to obey the laws before they can become American citizens.

Write About It Write a letter telling what you think a good citizen of any country should know.

105

C CHRISTIANITY

When Augustus was emperor, a child named Jesus was born in the province of Judea. This young Jewish boy would grow into a man whose ideas would greatly affect the world.

Jesus' Teachings

The New Testament of the Christian Bible has many stories of the life and teachings of Jesus and his followers. Around A.D. 30, Jesus left his home in Nazareth and, for three years, traveled Judea preaching and explaining his ideas.

Some believed Jesus to be a leader called the Messiah, sent by God to rule the world with peace. Messiah in Greek is *Christos*, and Jesus' followers became known as Christians.

▲ A Roman mosaic of Jesus

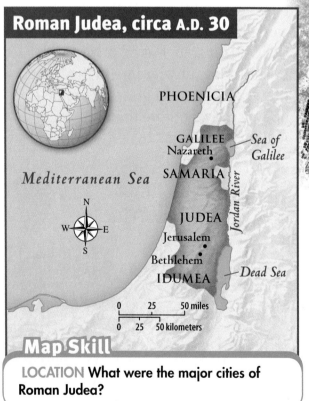

Roman Judea, circa A.D. 30

PHOENICIA

Mediterranean Sea

GALILEE
Nazareth

Sea of Galilee

SAMARIA

Jordan River

JUDEA

Jerusalem

Bethlehem

IDUMEA

Dead Sea

0   25   50 miles
0   25   50 kilometers

Map Skill

LOCATION **What were the major cities of Roman Judea?**

Jesus' teachings often use parables, or simple stories that contain a message. Some of these stories taught the value of seeking the right path in life. Others describe the greatness of God's love, or stress the importance of loving all people. Many of these stories taught that God forgives mistakes and wants all people to turn away from bad deeds.

The Death of Jesus

Jesus' growing popularity troubled some people in power. They were afraid that Jesus wanted to be king of Judea. Such ideas worried the Roman governor, who feared a revolt. When Jesus came to Jerusalem to celebrate the Passover festival, the Romans arrested him. The Roman governor executed him by crucifixion, meaning "putting to death by hanging from a cross."

The New Testament says that Jesus rose from the dead three days after his crucifixion. Then, he rejoined his followers and told them again of the coming kingdom of God. Afterwards, the New Testament says, Jesus rose to heaven. Today, Christians celebrate his renewed life on Easter Sunday.

Christianity Grows

One man who helped to spread Christianity never even met Jesus. Saul of Tarsus grew up in what is now Turkey. He was well educated in Judaism and the Greek classics. At first he opposed Christianity, but later he became a Christian and changed his name to Paul. He spent the rest of his life spreading Jesus' message and founding churches throughout the eastern Mediterranean.

Around A.D. 60, Christianity began to draw the attention of the Roman empire. Some Roman rulers punished Christians because they would not worship the emperor. Christians were often willing to die rather than give up their beliefs. Despite these hardships, Christianity continued to spread.

A State Religion

In A.D. 311, the Roman emperor Constantine became a Christian. According to tradition, he believed the Christian God

had helped him win a civil war and become emperor. Constantine issued an order called the Edict of Milan. It gave religious freedom to all people in the empire and made Christianity legal. Constantine built Christian churches in Rome, Constantinople, and Jerusalem. One of his successors, the emperor Theodosius, made Christianity the official religion of the empire in A.D. 392.

QUICK CHECK

Fact and Opinion Use facts to explain the opinion that Roman leaders held about Christians.

107

D THE BYZANTINE EMPIRE

The Roman Empire in the east lasted almost a thousand years after the fall of Rome in A.D. 476. The population of the eastern empire was largely Greek, and its people spoke Greek. They continued the traditions of Hellenism and combined them with Christianity and the traditions of Rome.

The "Queen of Cities"

Constantinople grew rich from trade and manufacturing. Its walls were a marvel of engineering that stopped all attackers for nearly a thousand years. The city also had the largest church in the world, called Hagia Sophia, or "holy wisdom."

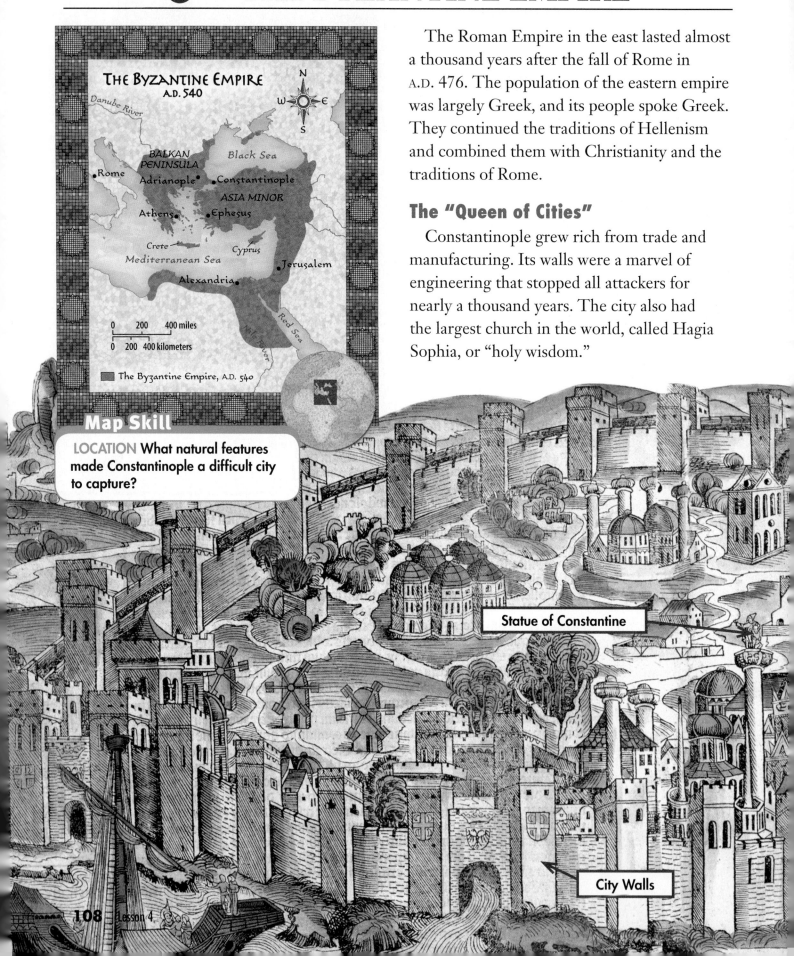

THE BYZANTINE EMPIRE
A.D. 540

Danube River

BALKAN PENINSULA
Black Sea
Rome
Adrianople
Constantinople
ASIA MINOR
Athens
Ephesus
Crete
Cyprus
Mediterranean Sea
Jerusalem
Alexandria
Red Sea
Nile River

0   200   400 miles
0 200 400 kilometers

The Byzantine Empire, A.D. 540

Map Skill

LOCATION What natural features made Constantinople a difficult city to capture?

Statue of Constantine

City Walls

Justinian the Great

In A.D. 527, Justinian became emperor in the east. Under Justinian, the Byzantine Empire reached its height. He expanded the borders of the empire and even tried to reconquer the lands of the Western Roman Empire. To support his government, Justinian demanded high taxes. In, 532, a revolt broke out in Constantinople. Justinian ruthlessly put down the revolt and reestablished power.

Justinian reorganized the laws of the Roman Empire. His code, or collection, of laws covered property, marriage, women, slaves, and criminals. The Justinian Code was the basis of Byzantine law and became very influential in shaping future legal systems.

A Split in the Church

There were almost constant arguments between Rome and Constantinople about religion. In 1054, the Church split. Eastern Christians became known as Orthodox Christians. The Byzantines sent missionaries to spread the Orthodox Church's beliefs to Russia, Africa, and throughout southwest Asia.

QUICK CHECK

Fact and Opinion Do you think Constantinople should have been called "the Queen of Cities"? Could you suggest another city? Support your opinion with facts.

Hagia Sophia

▲ A western European view of the walled city of Constantinople

Check Understanding

1. **VOCABULARY** Write about life in the Roman Empire during the rule of Augustus, using these vocabulary words.

   Pax Romana   **aqueduct**

   census   **inflation**

2. **READING SKILL Fact and Opinion** Use the completed chart from page 102 to write a paragraph explaining why Octavian was called Augustus, the "honored one."

Fact	Opinion

3. **Write About It** Explain the decline of the Roman Empire.

EXPLORE The Big Idea

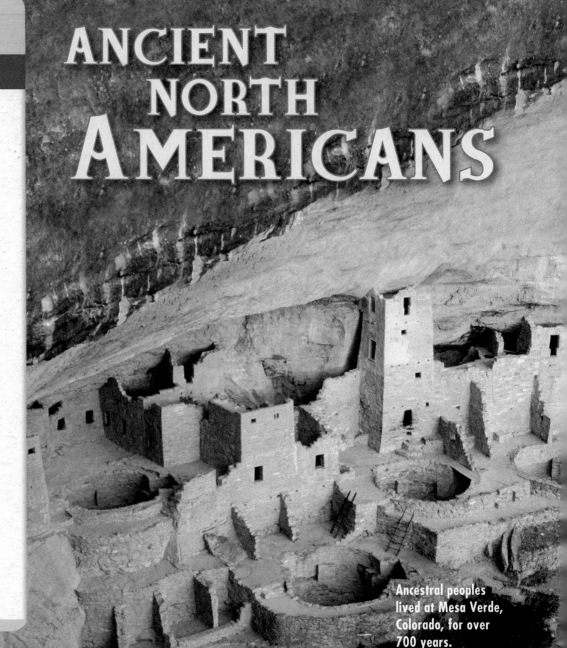

ANCIENT NORTH AMERICANS

Lesson 5

VOCABULARY

pueblo p. 112

adobe p. 113

totem p. 113

codex p. 117

glyph p. 117

READING SKILL

Fact and Opinion
Complete the chart with facts about the cultures of the Americas. Write two opinions based on each fact.

Fact	Opinion

New York Academic Content Standards

2.1, 2.2, 2.3, 3.1, 3.2

Ancestral peoples lived at Mesa Verde, Colorado, for over 700 years.

Visual Preview

How did early civilizations adapt to North America?

A Early Americans may have come across a land bridge from Asia.

B Early civilizations arose in the eastern woodlands and southwestern deserts.

C The Olmec civilization is called the "mother culture" of Mexico.

D The Maya civilization was the most successful in Middle America.

A A BRIDGE TO AMERICA

We have a lot of questions about the first humans in the Americas. How did they get here? Did they come 15,000 years ago or as much as 30,000 years ago? What can we learn from their artifacts?

Ancient hunters probably arrived in North America 15,000 to 30,000 years ago, during the last Ice Age. They may have come by boat across the Pacific Ocean from Asia. They may have come by boat from Europe. They may even have walked over from Europe and Asia across glaciers, or huge sheets of ice.

Many scientists believe the first Americans walked over a land bridge, called Beringia, that connected Asia and Alaska. During the Ice Age, ocean water turned to ice, and sea levels dropped about 300 feet. People could walk across the land that was uncovered. Animals most likely came over the land bridge, looking for new grazing lands. People followed the animals east and south across Beringia.

When the Ice Age ended, water again covered Beringia. By that time, people were already spreading out across the Americas and exploring their new home.

New Environments

Bison and deer spread out and led humans across what is today Canada, the United States, and Mexico. The first Americans would have found a swamp where Washington, D.C., sits today,

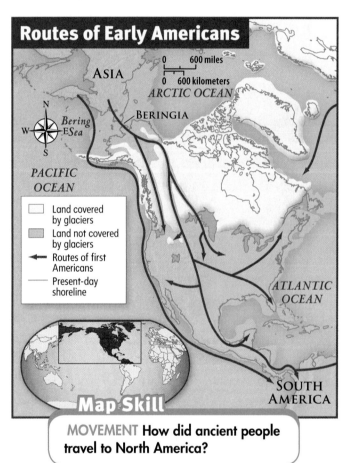

Routes of Early Americans

Land covered by glaciers
Land not covered by glaciers
← Routes of first Americans
— Present-day shoreline

Map Skill

MOVEMENT **How did ancient people travel to North America?**

and only trees where the skyscrapers of Manhattan now rise. Human cultures developed in every corner of what is now the United States.

QUICK CHECK

Fact and Opinion How do you think people first came to the Americas? What facts support this opinion?

111

EARLIEST AMERICANS

Ohio's Great Serpent Mound was constructed between A.D. 1000 and 1500. ▶

Centuries before the Pilgrims landed at Plymouth Rock, civilizations arose in the southwestern and eastern United States.

Southwest Peoples

Beneath the modern city of Phoenix, Arizona, is an ancient village. It was built by people called the Hohokam, meaning "those who have vanished." It is a name given by the groups that came after the Hohokam.

The Hohokam settled in the valleys of the Salt and Gila rivers around A.D. 300. Using only wooden and stone tools, the Hohokam built hundreds of miles of canals for irrigation. The canals were so well made that some are still used by farmers in the region today.

Desert Cities

The "four corners" region is where Colorado, New Mexico, Utah, and Arizona meet. Here lie the ruins of the Ancestral **Pueblo** civilization. They are called Ancestral because they were the ancestors of the Pueblo, Hopi, and Zuni cultures. Pueblo is a Spanish word meaning "people." Pueblo also describes the villages these people built.

The Ancestral Pueblo farmed with water from underground springs, summer rainstorms, and snow melt-off. These people grew corn, beans, and squash. During severe droughts, or dry spells, they hunted and gathered whatever the desert offered.

Around A.D. 1100, the Ancestral Pueblo began to build cliffside cities out of stone blocks, logs, and **adobe**—clay that has been formed into sun-dried bricks. These cliff cities could be reached only by ladders. The ladders could be pulled up in times of danger. The cliff cities had hundreds of rooms. It would be 700 years before buildings in North America would house as many people as these adobe towns.

By 1300, however, the Ancestral Pueblo cities were almost empty. War, or perhaps a drought, may have driven the people away. Not everyone left—descendants of one group have lived in New Mexico's Acoma Pueblo for 900 years. It is the oldest continuously occupied village in the United States.

Eastern Peoples

If you fly in a small plane across southern Ohio, you will see the Great Serpent Mound, which stretches 1,000 feet in the shape of a snake swallowing an egg. Other mounds, or human-made hills, are found from Florida in the south to Wisconsin in the north. The earliest mounds were constructed about 3,000 years ago. Historians think two groups, the Adena and the Hopewell, made most of these mounds.

The Adena are named after a site in Ohio where mounds were studied in the early 1900s. The Adena were hunter-gatherers who lived in small villages. They began building mounds in about 600 B.C. Their mounds covered tombs of important leaders. Later burials increased the size of mounds. Some were as high as 65 feet. Other mounds, shaped like birds, bears, turtles, or other animals, may have been **totems**, animal symbols of a group or family.

Hopewell culture is named for a family farm where a major mound was found. The Hopewell peoples came after the Adena and built even larger mounds and villages. The mound-building civilizations faded out around A.D. 1500. Historians are not sure of the reason, but it may have been due to a long period of cold weather.

QUICK CHECK

Cause and Effect What was the effect of desert geography on Ancestral Pueblo agriculture?

▲ Artifacts like this Hopewell hand and toad and the Adena human figure help historians understand the cultures that made them.

C THE OLMEC

In 1858, a worker struggled to clear the jungle near the Mexican village of Tres Zapotes. He came upon a gigantic stone and cleared away the plants and dirt. Glaring at him was a face carved in the giant rock.

The name Olmec means "people of the rubber country," because their area was full of rubber trees. We do not know what they called themselves, as Olmec was a name given to them by those who came after them. Around 1200 B.C., the Olmec began settling in the hot, wet region of thick rain forests. Here, trees soar 200 feet. Tangled vines twist around trees, and plants cover the forest floor.

Olmec Farmers

The Olmec began as hunter-gatherers. Later, they cleared their fields by using the slash-and-burn technique. They set a clearing on fire, then used the ash to fertilize the soil. The warm, wet climate allowed two or more harvests a year, so the Olmec produced more than enough food for their villages.

Maize, or corn, may have been planted in Middle America as early as 5000 B.C. It is still one of the world's most important crops.

Olmec Culture

Olmec cities grew into trading and religious centers. Olmec cities usually had a central square facing a flattened pyramid. On top of the pyramid was a temple.

The Olmec worshipped many gods. By about 800 B.C., the most powerful Olmec city was La Venta. At its center was the 100-foot-high Great Pyramid.

An Olmec carved head in a Mexican forest ▼

Olmec Lands
800 B.C.

N
W E
S

Gulf of Mexico

Tres Zapotes

Laguna de los Cerros

La Venta

San Lorenzo

PACIFIC OCEAN

0   100   200 miles
0   100   200 kilometers

☐ Olmec lands
• Olmec city

Map Skill

REGION **What are some characteristics of the region where the Olmec lived?**

▲ Maya women prepare traditional corn tortillas.

Tortillas

2 cups finely ground corn flour
1 1/3 cup warm water

1. Mix water and flour to make a soft dough.

2. Roll small balls of tortilla dough in your palms.

3. Flatten dough into very thin pancakes.

4. Have an adult place flattened tortilla on a hot griddle.

5. Cook for two minutes, turning tortilla once.

Jaguars often appear in Olmec carvings, and there are also many carvings of half-jaguar, half-human figures. Carvings also show a priest turning into a jaguar. The Olmec may have believed that priests took on the form of a jaguar before they were permitted to talk to the gods.

The Olmec carved "colossal heads" from a hard volcanic rock called basalt. Colossal means really big and massive. Sculptors used stone tools and bone drills to carve the stern faces. Each one is different and probably shows an individual Olmec ruler. Seventeen heads have been found so far. The largest stands 9 feet tall and weighs 24 tons.

Skilled Olmec workers made sharp knife blades of obsidian, a volcanic glass. The Olmec traded with other people to get the obsidian they needed. Archaeologists have found Olmec clay figures and other trade items as far as 300 miles from La Venta. Olmec traders spread Olmec customs and culture to other groups across Central America. As a result, the Olmec are often called the "mother culture" of this region.

The Olmec Decline

Around 400 B.C., something went wrong. We have no written records, so historians disagree. There may have been a flood, a drought, or a volcanic eruption. Were the Olmec attacked, or was there a civil war? Whatever happened caused the people to leave. Eventually, jungle swallowed La Venta—and Olmec history. They remained hidden for more than 2,000 years.

QUICK CHECK

Fact and Opinion Why do historians call the Olmec "the mother culture"? What facts support this opinion?

Six hundred years after the decline of the Olmec, the Maya civilization reached its peak. They lived in southern Mexico and the highlands of present-day Guatemala and Honduras. The Maya had lived in the area as early as 1000 B.C., and by A.D. 900 they had built a spectacular civilization.

Maya Civilization

Maya cities had tall, stepped pyramids made of huge stone blocks and topped with temples. Each king ordered a temple built, which became his tomb after his death. Artists carved pictures on walls or painted them as murals.

The Maya's main crop was maize. The god of maize often appears in Maya art, and one Maya myth tells how the people were molded from maize dough. The maize they grew, however, was smaller than modern ears of corn.

Religion was very important to the Maya. They worshiped hundreds of gods. For example, hunters, poets, and beekeepers each worshiped different gods. The king and other nobles led many of the religious ceremonies. The Maya also closely studied the stars and planets as part of their religion.

More Than a Game

Almost all Maya cities had a ball court, where young men from different cities played a fierce game called pok-ta-pok. Scholars think the game sometimes helped settle political problems between cities. Losing players in these games may have been put to death!

▲ The ball court at Chichén Itzá still has its stone ball hoop.

Pok-Ta-Pok Rules

1. The game is played with a 10-pound natural rubber ball on a rectangular ball court.

2. The game can be played as singles or by teams.

3. Players cannot touch the ball with their hands.

4. The ball may bounce twice, but then must be returned by the opposing team.

5. Points are scored by hitting the ball into the end zones.

6. If a player hits the ball through a narrow stone hoop, he or his team wins the game.

Writing and Numbers

The Maya had a written language as early as 300 B.C. Paper was made from the leaves of the agave plant or from dried animal skins. The sheets were folded into a long book called a **codex**. Spanish conquerors in the 1500s burned most of these writings. Only four codices—more than one codex—have survived, but they have helped historians to learn the Maya language.

The Maya language was written in **glyphs**, picture symbols like Egyptian hieroglyphics. Some represent objects and actions. Others stand for sounds and syllables. For many years, these could not be read. Recently, archaeologists have begun to find ways to translate Maya glyphs.

Maya writing describes the lives of their rulers. The earliest Maya painting tells a story about the maize god. Experts think this painting was made around 100 B.C. in Guatemala. The Maya also recorded important events on tall, flat stones called stelae. These stones were displayed in cities and marked historical events.

Maya mathematicians used other glyphs to create a number system. This was one of the first number systems to use a zero. The Maya

also developed an advanced calendar system. One calendar, the "Sacred Round," was made up of 13 cycles of 20 named days. This calendar had religious importance. Another calendar accurately followed the 365-day solar year. Maya astronomers could also predict eclipses.

Today, four million descendants of the Maya live in the region. Some Maya continue to use their calendar. Some speak the ancient Maya language and continue Maya customs.

QUICK CHECK

Fact and Opinion Use facts from the lesson to write an opinion about the Maya.

Check Understanding

1. **VOCABULARY** Write a summary of the Ancestral Pueblo people using each vocabulary word below.

   pueblo   **adobe**   **totem**

2. **READING SKILL Fact and Opinion** Use the chart from page 110 to write an opinion about the cultures of the Americas. Use facts to support your opinion.

Fact	Opinion

3. **Write About It** What do you believe about the rise and fall of early American cultures?

Lesson 6

VOCABULARY

causeway p. 120

terrace p. 122

hydroponics p. 124

quipu p. 124

READING SKILL

Fact and Opinion
Fill in the chart with facts and opinions about empires in the Americas.

Fact	Opinion

New York Academic Content Standards
2.1, 2.2, 2.3, 3.1, 3.2

TOLTEC, AZTEC, AND INCA

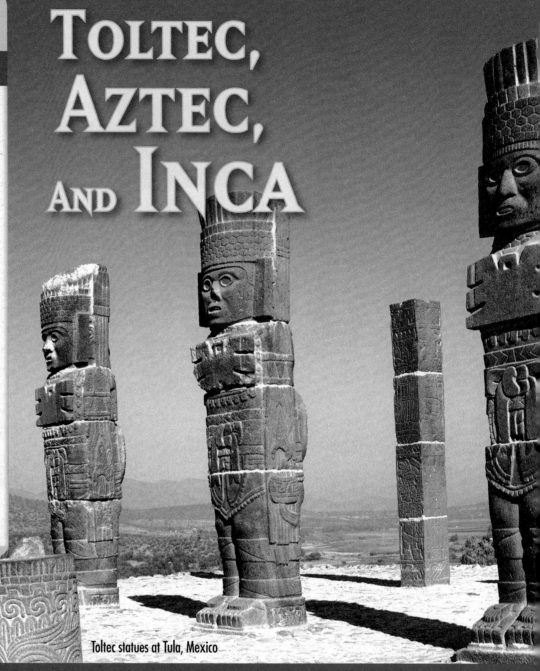

Toltec statues at Tula, Mexico

Visual Preview

How did empires develop in the Americas?

A The Toltec Empire developed in central Mexico.

B The Aztec built on older cultures in Mexico.

C The Inca built a large empire in the Andes Mountains.

D The Inca made advances as engineers, architects, and metalworkers.

THE TOLTEC EMPIRE

"When we saw all those cities and villages built in the water, and other great towns on dry land . . . we were astounded," wrote Bernal Díaz del Castillo, one of the Spanish soldiers who conquered the Aztec empire in the 1500s. "These great towns . . . seemed like an enchanted vision."

The Toltec people are another ancient people of Mexico. They began as hunter-gatherers, but, around A.D. 900, they settled in central Mexico. Within a century, the Toltec controlled a large part of what is today Mexico.

The Toltec Culture

Much of what we know about the Toltec comes from the records of people who lived in the same region many years later. In fact, we are not even sure that they called themselves Toltec.

We do know that their capital was the city of Tula. Archaeologists have investigated the ruins of Tula. Most of our knowledge comes from the Aztec, however, who came after the Toltec.

The people of Tula seem to have been the first to worship a feathered serpent called Quetzalcoatl. They believed this god left Mexico one day but promised to return at a later time. The Aztec also worshipped Quetzalcoatl. Pictures of this god can be found on ancient artifacts.

Around A.D. 1200, the Toltec Empire was conquered. Again, there are few written stories about them, but it seems that a civil war broke out and enemies took the opportunity to overthrow the Toltec rulers. The Toltec Empire was eventually replaced by the Aztec. You will read about them on the next page.

QUICK CHECK

Fact and Opinion What facts do we have about the fall of the Toltec Empire? What is your opinion about how their empire fell?

Chacmool, the Maya god of rain ▼

bowl for offerings

THE AZTEC GAIN POWER

The Aztec, or Mexica, arrived in central Mexico around A.D. 1200 and settled on an island in Lake Texcoco. The Aztec had a myth which said they should settle where they saw an eagle on a cactus holding a snake. Legend says on this site they built Tenochtitlán.

Building Tenochtitlán

By the early 1500s, about 200,000 people were living in Tenochtitlán, making it one of the largest cities in the world at that time. Earthen roadways called **causeways** reached the shore. The city center had large temples, palaces, schools, and houses for priests.

The Valley of Mexico did not have good farmland. This led the Aztec to create *chinampas*, or artificial islands, on Lake Texcoco. Farmers filled reed baskets with rich lake mud. Then, they planted crops in the reed baskets and tied them in place.

The Aztec Empire

When the Aztec first settled in the Valley of Mexico, they had to pay tribute, or taxes, to their powerful neighbors. In 1428, the Aztec army joined with two nearby cities and took control of the valley. By the early 1500s, the Aztec Empire had expanded west to the Pacific Ocean and south to present-day Guatemala.

The Aztec knew how to make objects of gold and silver, but they did not work with iron. Instead, their weapons had sharp blades made of obsidian. Aztec warriors wore armor of quilted cotton that had been soaked in vinegar to make it hard.

◄ Aztec calendar stone with the sun god at the center

Aztec Culture

The Aztec worshiped many gods, including a war and sun god, a rain god, and a corn goddess. They also worshiped the Aztec ruler because they believed he was related to the gods. Human sacrifice was part of the Aztec religion. The Aztec hoped to gain the protection of their gods by giving them human lives. On the top of the Great Pyramid, Aztec priests sacrificed thousands of war prisoners.

Aztec science and technology were advanced. Doctors had medicines and plants used to heal wounds, reduce fevers, and cure stomach aches. Aztec astronomers developed an accurate calendar. A "sun calendar" was carved in stone with images of historical events. It was also used to predict solar eclipses.

Aztec writing used symbols and pictures to record their history, religious beliefs, and scientific ideas. The Spanish destroyed most of the Aztec codices, but a few have survived. Also, several Aztec songs, poems, and stories have been passed down through oral tradition.

Mexican Heritage

Mexicans today have many reminders of their Aztec heritage. For example, the Mexican flag shows the eagle holding the snake from the Aztec legend. Aztec artistic styles are still used by Mexican artists. Some people in central Mexico still speak the Aztec language. In fact, the name "Mexico" comes from the name the Aztec called themselves—Mexica.

QUICK CHECK

Cause and Effect Before establishing their empire, what did the Aztec have to do?

◄ Pyramid of the Moon, Teotihuacán, Mexico

THE RISE OF THE INCA

South America is a land of extreme geography. This continent has the world's longest river, the Amazon. It also has the world's longest mountain range, the Andes.

The Andes stretch down the western coast of South America, like the continent's backbone. The Andes chain is about 4,500 miles long. Life can be difficult in the dry, rugged, and cold Andes. There are frequent earthquakes and volcanic eruptions. Travel is difficult. To cross the canyons, early people built sturdy rope bridges.

Early farmers in the Andes dug canals to irrigate their farms. Where the land was steeper, they planted on **terraces**, flat areas dug out of the hillsides. The Inca capital was Cuzco, Peru. Cuzco sat high in the mountains at the heart of the empire. Today, Cuzco is home to more than 300,000 people.

Like the Aztec, the Inca settled in an area that had been home to earlier civilizations. The Inca borrowed ideas from these earlier cultures. Later, they created an empire along the west coast of South America.

Inca Accomplishments

In 1438, Pachakuti became the Inca ruler. He sent his soldiers out to conquer vast areas. Everyone in the empire worked for the central government. Men farmed and built roads while women made cloth. People were fed and clothed from central storehouses.

The Inca Empire grew to include about 12 million people. Cuzco became a rich and powerful city. It was the center of government, religion, and trade. Government and religious buildings near the city center were constructed from stone.

Skilled builders cut stone and constructed temples, forts, and palaces without using cement. These blocks fit together so well that it is impossible to put a knife between them. The buildings were good at surviving earthquakes, and many of their walls are still standing. The Inca also built thousands of miles of roads. Armies and supplies could be rushed along these roads. Messengers traveled quickly across the empire, bringing news to the Inca ruler.

terrace

Children of the Sun

The most important Inca god was Inti, the sun god. The Inca considered themselves "the children of the sun." They believed that their rulers were related to the sun and worshiped them as well. The Inca worshiped many other gods, including an Earth goddess, a sea goddess, a god of thunder, and a rainbow god.

The Inca worked rich gold mines. They called this metal "sweat of the sun" and used it to decorate temples to their sun god. His temple in Cuzco had a huge golden sculpture of him decorated with precious stones.

PEOPLE

The name **Pachakuti** means "earthquake." He was a great general and organizer. He commanded armies, planned harvests, and constructed roads, dams, terraces, canals, and buildings.

Pachakuti

QUICK CHECK

Fact and Opinion What are some of your opinions about the Inca? Are your opinions based on fact?

◄ Women walk beside a terraced hillside in modern Peru.

The Inca had three rules: *Ama suwa, Ama quella, Ama llulla.* Do not steal, do not be lazy, do not lie. Inca society was strictly organized. Everyone worked for the state, which provided clothing and food for everyone.

The Inca emperor was at the top of the social pyramid. Under him were nobles and priests. Next were conquered rulers and chiefs. They still kept some of their power and served as regional judges. The largest social group was made up of peasants.

The emperor, nobles, and priests lived on or near the great plaza at the center of Cuzco. Many temples and government buildings were located here. Farmers and other workers lived with their families in simple homes built of mud bricks, stone, or reeds.

Farmers grew potatoes, corn, and peppers. They farmed terraces along hillsides. Farmers also grew crops by using **hydroponics**. This is a method of growing crops in water. The water supplies the nutrients the crops need. In dry areas, farmers used irrigation canals to water their crops. The Inca were expert farmers who fed roughly 12 million people in a region that is not well suited to agriculture.

The Inca Empire circa A.D. 1530

Amazon River

Maranon R.

Cajamarca

Chancay

Machu Picchu

Cuzco

Lake Titicaca

SOUTH AMERICA

PACIFIC OCEAN

ANDES MOUNTAINS

| 0 | 300 | 600 miles |
| 0 | 300 | 600 kilometers |

Inca lands
City

Map Skill

REGION **How did the Andes Mountains affect the Inca Empire?**

Records of Thread

The Inca did not have an alphabet or the usual kind of written language. They were able to keep records with **quipus**. A quipu was a set of colored and knotted strings.

A quipu was about two feet long. The colors of the threads indicated news. For example, white threads stood for silver. Yellow threads meant gold. Red threads indicated war. By tying knots in a particular order, the quipu could be "read." The Inca used the quipu to record population, taxes, and events.

PLACES

Pachakuti ordered the fortress city of **Machu Picchu** to be built high in the Andes. The Inca abandoned Machu Picchu around the same time the Spanish invaded. It was rediscovered in 1911.

Machu Picchu

▲ An Inca quipu and a bird of gold and turquoise against a woven cape from Peru

We know from Spanish records that the Inca created beautiful works of art. Many sculptures were made of gold and silver. The Inca called gold the "sweat of the sun" and silver the "tears of the moon." The Spanish melted most of these sculptures for their gold or silver after the fall of the Inca Empire.

A Living Language

One thing that did survive the Spanish conquest is the Inca language, Quechua. While a large number of people in the Andes speak Spanish, millions of people in the Andes region continue to speak Quechua today. Speakers of Quechua live in the South American nations of Argentina, Bolivia, Chile, Colombia, Ecuador, and Peru.

QUICK CHECK

Cause and Effect How did roads build unity in the Inca Empire?

Check Understanding

1. **VOCABULARY** Write a summary of what you learned in this lesson using the following vocabulary words.

   | causeway | hydroponics |
   | terrace | quipu |

2. **READING SKILL Fact and Opinion** Use the chart from page 118 to write your opinions about the empires in the Americas. Support your opinions with facts from this lesson.

Fact	Opinion

3. **Write About It** How did technology help the Aztec and the Inca build large empires?

125

Vocabulary

Write a word from the list that best completes each sentence.

harbor   tyrant   civil war

inflation   adobe

1. The _____ seized power.

2. Workers need sand and straw to make _____.

3. The boats found shelter in the _____ during the storm.

4. The generals fought a _____ to control the empire.

5. _____ makes prices shoot upward and money is worth less.

Comprehension and Critical Thinking

6. How is a republic different from a democracy?

7. What are some characteristics of the "Pax Romana"?

8. **Reading Skill** How did Constantine change the history of the Roman Empire?

9. **Critical Thinking** Why might Augustus have carefully kept up the ideas of the republic after he became emperor?

10. **Critical Thinking** How do we know that the Inca were great organizers?

Skill

Historical Maps

Write a complete sentence to answer each question.

11. Which Maya site is farthest north?

12. What was the approximate north-south length and east-west width of Maya lands?

Mesoamerica, A.D. 250–900

95°W   90°W

0   75   150 miles
0   75   150 kilometers

Chichén Itzá

Tulum   20°N

Gulf of Mexico

YUCATÁN PENINSULA

Palenque

Tikal

Yaxchilan

Bonampak

15°N

PACIFIC OCEAN

☐ Maya land
■ Maya site

New York English Language Arts Test Preparation

Directions
Read this passage about Greece. Then answer questions 1 and 2.

Greece is a mountainous peninsula on the European coast of the Mediterranean Sea. A peninsula is an area of land bordered by water on three sides. Actually, the Greek peninsula is made up of two peninsulas. Attica is on the east and the Peloponnesus is to the south. Mountains make overland travel difficult, so ancient Greeks never united into one country.

---

1 What is the main idea of this passage?

   A Greece's geography

   B Greek culture

   C Greece's climate

   D Greek food

2 What body of water surrounds Greece?

   A Peloponnesian Sea

   B Attica

   C Peloponnesus

   D Mediterranean Sea

The Big Idea Activities

Why do empires rise and fall?

Write About the Big Idea

Persuasive Essay
Use the Unit 2 foldable to help you write a persuasive essay. Answer the Big Idea question, Why do empires rise and fall? Begin your essay with a statement of your opinion. Use your foldable for details to support each main idea. End with a concluding paragraph that summarizes your opinion.

FOLDABLES™
Study Organizer

Empires Rise and Fall

Greece | Rome | Americas

Make a Poster

Work independently to prepare a poster. The subject will be "Seven Wonders of Empires." Here's how to make your poster:

1. Research the accomplishments of Greece, Rome, and the Americas.

2. Choose seven buildings or other large construction projects from all three empires.

3. Draw a picture or find a photo to illustrate each of your choices.

4. Write a description of each of your choices.

5. Present your poster to your class. Be sure to explain why you chose each of your selections.

Unit 3

For more about Unit 3, go to
www.macmillanmh.com

Essential Question
How do cultures influence each other?

FOLDABLES
Study Organizer

Summarize
Use this layered book foldable to take notes as you read Unit 3. Label it **The Arab Empire, The Ottoman Empire, East African Empires,** and **African Trading Empires.**

The Arab Empire
The Ottoman Empire
East African Empires
African Trading Empires

Fruit and vegetable vendor in the Luxor Souq, Egypt, Africa

Trade and Tradition

PEOPLE, PLACES, AND EVENTS

Piye

Meroë

728 B.C. | Piye conquers Egypt

Mansa Musa

Tombouctou

A.D.1312 | Mansa Musa becomes king of Mali

700 BC   AD 1250   AD 1300

King Piye of Kush conquered all of Egypt by 728 B.C. His army's use of war elephants filled its enemies with fear.

Today visitors to **Meroë**, Sudan, can see the remains of dozens of Kushite pyramids.

In 1324 king **Mansa Musa** of Mali made a pilgrimage to the holy Muslim city of Makkah, along with 60,000 people, and tons of gold.

Today you can see buildings from Mansa's time in **Tombouctou**, Mali.

Ibn Batuta

Baghdad

A.D.1325

Ibn Batuta
begins his
travels

Mehmet II

Constantinople

A.D.1453

Mehmet II
conquers
Constantinople

AD 1350   AD 1400   AD 1450

In 1325 **Ibn Batuta** began a 29-year, 75,000-mile journey around the world, visiting great cities like the Muslim capital, Baghdad.

Today visitors to **Baghdad**, Iraq, can see some of the same sights that attracted Ibn Batuta.

In 1453 **Mehmet II** and his army conquered Constantinople by pounding its walls with a new weapon—the cannon.

Today you can see Mehmet's prize by visiting the city of **Istanbul**, Turkey.

VOCABULARY

oasis p. 133

caravan p. 135

Muslim p. 136

pilgrimage p. 137

READING SKILL

Summarize
What were the major events in the life of Muhammad?

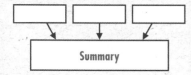

↓ ↓ ↓

Summary

New York Academic Content Standards
1.4, 2.1, 2.2, 2.3, 3.1, 3.2

The Arab World

The Sahara Desert

How did the growth of Islam change Arabia?

A People have lived on the Arabian Peninsula for thousands of years.

B Early Arab civilizations flourished in harsh desert regions.

C Islam developed on the Arabian Peninsula starting in A.D. 610.

D Muslims believe that the Quran holds Allah's teachings as given to Muhammad.

A | THE ARABIAN PENINSULA

The desert areas of the Arabian Peninsula are some of the hottest, driest places in the world. Much of the region gets less than seven inches of rain a year. Yet people have lived in Arabia for thousands of years.

The southwest Asian region known as the Arabian Peninsula, or just Arabia, has some of the world's largest, driest desert areas. Some of these have gone for 10 years or more with no rain. One is the well-named *Rub´ al Khali*—"the Empty Quarter." Fortunately, the Jabal al-Hijaz Mountains on the west coast receive enough rainfall to make agriculture possible, as does the peninsula's east coast.

Arabia's natural resources include gold, silver, sulfur, and salt, as well as about one-third of the world's petroleum and natural gas reserves. Those fuels are found mostly near the Persian Gulf. Today there are seven countries on the Arabian Peninsula. Saudi Arabia is the largest.

Living in the Desert

Much of Arabia is a dry desert, yet it has fertile areas that can support life. Parts of the desert are steppes, dry plains where some grasses and plants can grow. These provide enough grazing land for herds of sheep and goats. The desert also has a few oases. An **oasis** is a place in a desert with a dependable water supply. Early desert peoples traveled in groups from oasis to oasis with their animals to find water and grazing areas.

The Arabian Peninsula is named for the Arab people, who have lived there for more than 3,000 years. The term "Arab" was first recorded around 800 B.C. It referred to people from northern Arabia who used camels to travel around the region. The Arab name for the peninsula is *Jazirat al' Arab*, or "Island of the Arabs."

QUICK CHECK

Summarize How were people able to build agricultural civilizations in Arabia?

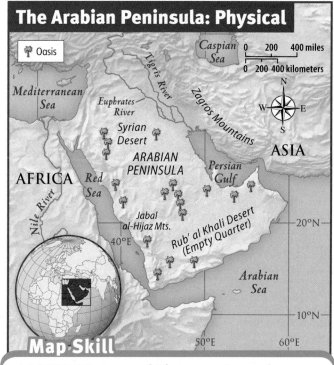

The Arabian Peninsula: Physical

Oasis

Mediterranean Sea
Caspian Sea
Tigris River
Euphrates River
Zagros Mountains
Syrian Desert
ARABIAN PENINSULA
Persian Gulf
ASIA
AFRICA
Red Sea
Nile River
Jabal al-Hijaz Mts.
Rub' al Khali Desert (Empty Quarter)
Arabian Sea
40°E
50°E
60°E
20°N
10°N

0 200 400 miles
0 200 400 kilometers

N W E S

Map Skill

LOCATION Between which two continents does Arabia lie?

Ⓑ EARLY ARAB CIVILIZATIONS

One group that settled in the region's fertile areas formed the Sabaean civilization. They lived in the mountainous region that is now the country of Yemen. Like early peoples in other mountain regions, the Sabaeans herded sheep and goats and grew grapes and wheat. They also dug canals to improve irrigation and increase their harvests. The Sabaeans traded with the Egyptians across the Red Sea.

Busy Traders

A second early civilization, Nabataea, was established around 300 B.C. in what is now Jordan. Nabataea's capital was the ancient city of Petra. Petra was in a perfect location for the Nabataeans to control trade routes between Asia and the Mediterranean Sea. As the busy spice trade made Petra wealthy, the Nabataeans were able to farm larger areas.

Petra had a steady supply of water delivered by aqueducts, very similar to those used in ancient Rome. They also developed new methods to conserve water. They stored rainwater behind dams and constructed underground cisterns, or tanks. Two thousand years ago, the Nabataeans were able to store millions of gallons of water in an area that today is uninhabited because of lack of water. At the time, one had to travel hundreds of miles south of Petra to find another city with a steady water supply.

This Nabataean building, known as El Deir, is 157 feet high. ▼

Nabataeans also depended on the camel. This humped, long-necked mammal requires little water to survive. Camels can also carry heavy loads and provide milk to drink. Arab traders led caravans of camels through the peninsula to the Fertile Crescent and Egypt. A **caravan** is a group of people who travel over trading routes by camel or horse.

The Nabataeans managed to turn a desert oasis into a thriving civilization. It was absorbed by the Roman Empire in A.D. 106. Petra remained an important trading center until A.D. 200.

Desert Travelers

The Bedouins were another group of traders that emerged in Arabia. Their name means "people of the desert." The Bedouins lived mostly in desert areas, traveling in caravans with their families and sleeping in tents along the way. Early Bedouins ate mostly dried fruits and nuts. They rarely ate meat, because their animals were too valuable to be used as food. This lifestyle is still followed by many Bedouins across the Middle East and North Africa today.

Trade helped the Bedouins and other Arabs thrive in a harsh environment. Merchants began settling in towns along Arabia's major trade routes. The city of Makkah soon became the largest of these towns, as well as a major religious center. Geography and culture divided different Arab groups until around A.D. 600, when a new religion united Arabia and changed the region forever.

QUICK CHECK

Summarize How did Petra become a major trading center?

Bedouin men in Egypt ▼

135

THE LIFE OF MUHAMMAD

By A.D. 600, several religions were practiced in Asia, North Africa, and Europe. Hinduism was common across India. Buddhism had spread from India to China and Southeast Asia. Christianity extended to parts of North Africa, Europe, and Mesopotamia. Judaism was also practiced from the Fertile Crescent south to Arabia. Soon a new religion called Islam would emerge on the Arabian Peninsula. The rapid growth in the number of Islam's followers, or **Muslims**, affected the entire region.

Muhammad the Prophet

Muhammad was born in the oasis city of Makkah in about A.D. 570. He was orphaned as a boy and raised by an uncle who was a trader. Muhammad grew up to be a respected caravan leader. His skills came to the attention of a wealthy widow and merchant named Khadija. Working for her, Muhammad traveled to the Fertile Crescent to trade goods. When he returned from his journey, they were married.

Muhammad had time to devote himself to thinking about religion. He was about 40 years old when he went to a mountain cave to pray. According to Islamic tradition, there he had a vision of the angel Gabriel who appeared and said, "O Muhammad, you are the prophet of Allah." *Allah* is the Arabic word for God. Muslims believe Allah is the same God worshiped by Jews and Christians.

Madinah
Makkah

Makkah and the Kaaba

The city of Makkah lay on the main trading route through western Arabia. It attracted traders and religious travelers. They came to pray at the Kaaba, Makkah's cube-shaped temple. Inside the Kaaba was a sacred black stone and the statues of the gods and goddesses that many Arabs worshiped at the time.

The Kaaba in Makkah, surrounded by worshippers

Muhammad was determined to persuade the people of Makkah to abandon their worship of many gods and goddesses. He told people to destroy statues of false gods and worship only Allah. He preached that all people are equal and that the rich should share their wealth with the poor. Over the next three years, Muhammad's group of followers slowly grew. They called themselves *Muslims*, or one who submits to the will of Allah.

From Makkah to Madinah

Muhammad soon aroused the anger of Makkah's leaders. They were worried that people would stop worshipping at the Kaaba, and that the leaders would then lose their wealth and power. Because of this, Muhammad and his followers were treated harshly. In 622 Muhammad's problems with Makkah's leaders forced him and his followers to flee the city.

In 622 Muhammad led his followers to settle in the town of Yathrib, about 200 miles north of Makkah. Later, the town's name would be changed to Madinah, or "city of the prophet." Muslims call his 200-mile journey to Madinah the *hijrah*, which is the Arabic word for migration. 622 later became the first year of the Muslim calendar. Muhammad stayed in Madinah for six years, organizing a Muslim community, government, and army.

Makkah's leaders were upset about the success of Muhammad and his followers in Madinah. Battles broke out between the two cities and, in A.D. 630, an army of Muslims captured Makkah. When Muhammad entered the city he destroyed the statues in the Kaaba and dedicated the shrine to the worship of Allah alone. He also declared Makkah to be a holy city, which it remains today.

▲ Muslim houses of worship have small nooks which face in the direction of Makkah.

Islam Grows

Muhammad returned to Madinah to live. He and his followers worked to unite Arabia under Islam. In 632 Muhammad and thousands of his followers returned to Makkah one last time on a **pilgrimage**, a long journey to a holy place or shrine. He died three months later. Just before his death, Muslims believe, Muhammad said to his followers: "Muslim believers are brothers of one another."

QUICK CHECK

Summarize How did Muhammad help spread the ideas of Islam throughout Arabia?

Ⓓ THE RELIGION OF ISLAM

After Muhammad's death, his teachings were written down by his followers in what became the holy book of Islam. This book, called the Quran, was completed around 651. Muslims consider it to be the literal words of Allah as revealed to Muhammad. The Quran serves as a guide for Muslims, as the Hebrew Bible does for Jews and the Christian Bible does for Christians. Through its words, Muslims learn about Allah's teachings. It remains the most important book in Islam to this day.

Primary Sources

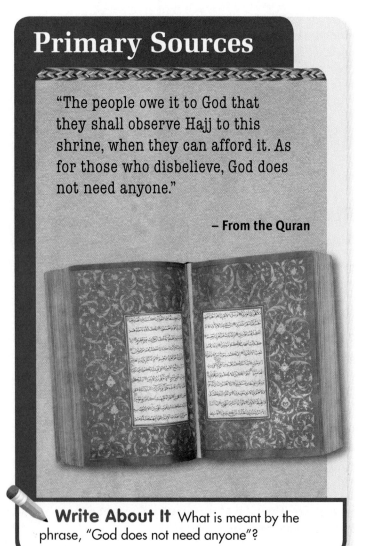

"The people owe it to God that they shall observe Hajj to this shrine, when they can afford it. As for those who disbelieve, God does not need anyone."

– From the Quran

✏️ **Write About It** What is meant by the phrase, "God does not need anyone"?

The Five Pillars

The Quran explains five basic duties of all Muslims. The purpose of these duties, known as the Five Pillars of Islam, is to strengthen the lives of Muslims and their communities. These duties are:

1. Shahadah — Testify, or say, that there is no God but Allah, and that Muhammad is Allah's prophet.

2. Salat — Make prayers at five specific times each day, always facing in the direction of Makkah.

3. Zakat — Give a small part of one's earnings to take care of the needy, the poor, those in debt, or those who are travelling.

4. Sawm — Fast, which means no eating or drinking from dawn to sunset during the holy month of Ramadan. Ramadan is the ninth month of the Muslim calendar. This pillar comes from the Muslim belief that Muhammad received the first of Allah's teachings during Ramadan. At the end of Ramadan, Muslims celebrate the holiday of Eid al-Fitr, or the Feast of the Fast.

5. Hajj — Make a Hajj, or religious pilgrimage to Makkah, during one's lifetime, if one can afford it. Another major Muslim holiday, Eid al-Adha, or the Feast of Sacrifice, marks the last day of the annual pilgrimage to Makkah. That city remains the spiritual center of Islam today, and more than two million Muslims go there during the Hajj season each year, which usually takes place in December. For more, see the Primary Source box on the left of this page.

▲ Children in Qatar mark the holy month of Ramadan.

Islam Today

In the 100 years after the death of Muhammed in 632, Islam spread and flourished. By 750, people living in lands from Spain to the Indus Valley in India had become Muslims. A Muslim empire had been established by Muhammed's followers. You will read about this empire in the next lesson.

Today there are more than a billion Muslims worldwide, including almost five million in the United States. Some Islamic customs and practices vary from community to community, but most Muslim families celebrate the end of Ramadan with Eid al-Fitr. During this holiday, children dress in new clothes and receive gifts. Families gather together and share a special meal that often includes sweet foods made with dates and honey.

There is no organized body of Muslim religious leaders. Each community chooses its own clergy. Millions of Muslims from around the world still make the pilgrimage to the holy city of Makkah every year. Muslims view the pilgrimage as one of the most important and spiritually rewarding events in their lives.

QUICK CHECK

Summarize **What are the Five Pillars of Islam?**

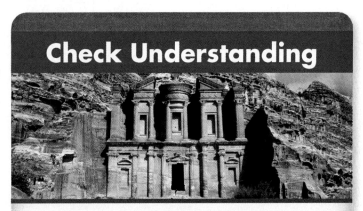

Check Understanding

1. **VOCABULARY** Write a paragraph about early Arab civilizations using the following words.

   oasis   caravan

2. **READING SKILL Summarize** Use your chart from page 132 to summarize the major events in the life of Muhammad.

 3. **Write About It** How did the growth of Islam change Arabia?

Lesson 2

VOCABULARY

caliph p. 141

bazaar p. 144

mosque p. 145

minaret p. 145

astrolabe p. 146

READING SKILL

Summarize

What were the most important achievements of the Muslim empire?

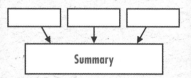

New York Academic Content Standards

2.1, 2.2, 2.3, 3.1, 3.2

The Muslim Empire

The Alhambra Palace in Spain

Visual Preview

How did the Muslim empire change the places it conquered?

A The Muslim empire spread across western Asia, North Africa, and into Spain.

B Many in the empire became Muslims, but other religions were allowed.

C People exchanged goods and ideas in the empire's capital, Baghdad.

D Muslim advances in science and medicine influenced other civilizations.

A MUSLIM EMPIRE

As the influence of Islam grew on the Arabian Peninsula, the Persian and Byzantine empires were declining. Soon after Muhammad's death, Muslim armies spread into Persia, the Fertile Crescent, North Africa, and Spain. By A.D. 700, Muhammad's followers controlled an empire.

After Muhammad died in 632, Muslim leaders selected caliphs, or successors, to govern the Muslim community. A **caliph** is a political and military ruler who lives by Muhammad's example and follows the teachings of the Quran.

Arabia's first four caliphs united Arabia under Islam and their rule. Once this had been accomplished, the caliphs set out to spread Islam—and their empire—in neighboring lands. By 651, they had conquered Persia, Egypt, and much of North Africa.

As the Muslim empire grew, these early caliphs organized a navy; built roads, bridges, and canals; created a code of conduct for their soldiers; and distributed the Quran throughout their new territories. Their empire became known as the caliphate. By 760, it stretched across North Africa and into parts of the Indus River Valley and China.

The Caliphate in Europe

The caliphs wanted to expand into Europe. Muslim forces from North Africa, also known as Moors, conquered present-day Spain and Portugal. These would remain Muslim territory for almost 600 years. Under Muslim rule, the Spanish city of Córdoba became the second-largest city in Europe and a major center of trade, architecture, and religion. Some of the greatest philosophers of this period lived in Muslim Spain.

The caliphate never expanded in Europe beyond Spain or Portugal. In 732 Muslim soldiers invaded present-day France, but they were defeated by troops led by Charles Martel. In the next unit, you will read about Martel's grandson, Charlemagne, and his empire in Europe.

QUICK CHECK

Summarize What did the caliphs who came after Muhammad accomplish?

PLACES

The reddish Alhambra palace in **Granada** was built bewtween 1248 and 1354 on a plateau overlooking the city. Today it is a museum of art from the time of the caliphate.

The Alhambra Palace

ISLAM AND THE CALIPHATE

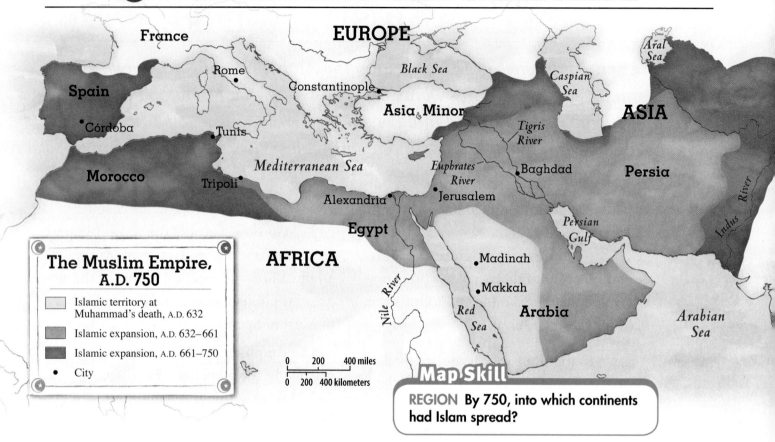

The Muslim Empire, A.D. 750

Islamic territory at Muhammad's death, A.D. 632

Islamic expansion, A.D. 632–661

Islamic expansion, A.D. 661–750

• City

0   200   400 miles
0   200 400 kilometers

Map Skill

REGION **By 750, into which continents had Islam spread?**

Caliphs believed that they were on a holy mission to spread Islam through conquest. In some places, people welcomed the Muslim troops. They hoped that Muslim rulers would be better than their old rulers.

Pilgrims traveling to Makkah ▼

When Muslims conquered a new land, they met people with many different beliefs and lifestyles. Some were allowed to practice their own religion. Christians and Jews were considered to be "people of the Book," because they shared the Muslim belief in one God and had their own holy books. As a result, they were allowed to practice their religion. Those who practiced religions other than Christianity or Judaism, however, faced persecution.

Even though Christians and Jews were treated with tolerance, Muslims did not treat them as equals. There were different laws for Muslims and non-Muslims in the empire. Non-Muslims Christians had to pay higher taxes than Muslims, swear to be loyal to their Muslim rulers, and promise not to try to convert anyone to their own religions.

A Split in Islam

As the Muslim empire grew, its leaders began to argue about how new caliphs should be chosen. This dispute led to a split in Islam that still exists today. One group of Muslims, the Shiites, believe that caliphs should be descendants of Muhammad. The second group, the Sunnis, do not believe that caliphs need to be related to Muhammad. Today the majority of Muslims worldwide are Sunnis. Most Shiites today live in the nation of Iran.

Muslim Society

Islam, like most religions, has a set of rules. In its beginnings Islam offered women some rights that were uncommon at the time. Women could inherit wealth and own property. They also could earn their own money and seek divorce. Many places had laws requiring women to cover their faces and to wear long robes in public.

Muslim people as a whole were split into different social groups based on power and wealth. At the top of society were government rulers like the caliph, followed by landowners and merchants. In the middle were craftspeople, laborers, and farmers. At the bottom of society were slaves.

The Quran does not forbid slavery, but it suggests that it should not be practiced. Under the caliphate, however, slavery was a part of life, as it was in many societies at the time. Some Muslims enslaved non-Muslims captured during battles. African and Turkish prisoners often became soldiers enslaved to the caliphate. According to Islamic law, many of these soldiers were freed after a certain number of years as slaves.

QUICK CHECK

Summarize How did the caliphate practice religious tolerance?

A decorated mosque in Isfahan, Iran ▶

ⓒ BAGHDAD CIVILIZATION

In 762 the caliph al-Mansur selected a spot along the Tigris River, in today's Iraq, to build the caliphate's capital. He called it Baghdad.

Baghdad's location along the Tigris was ideal for trade. Traders came to the city from around the world to exchange Arabian perfumes, Indian pepper, African ivory, Chinese dishes, and Russian furs in marketplaces called bazaars. A **bazaar** is a large market with rows of shops and tents. As Baghdad's population topped one million, it became one of the world's largest cities and a major center of science and culture as well.

Arab Learning

The caliphate valued learning and culture. Its leaders borrowed the best ideas of the people they conquered. They learned paper-making from Chinese prisoners in 751. Soon, printers across the empire began producing cookbooks, poems, and collections of stories. Baghdad had 36 public libraries, where people read books of poetry and collections of stories like *The Arabian Nights*. In that book, a cruel king tells a wise princess that he will kill her after their wedding. She distracts him by telling him a different story each night, for 1,001 nights.

An outdoor bazaar ▼

As the caliphate spread Islam far from Arabia, it also spread the Arabic language. By creating a common language over such a large territory, the caliphate could share literature, as well as philosophical and scientific ideas. During the centuries that followed, ideas developed in the caliphate would influence scientists, writers, and thinkers in Europe and spark a great wave of creative thinking.

In Baghdad's largest library, the House of Wisdom, scholars translated ancient Roman, Hebrew, and Indian texts into Arabic. Through their work, these scholars brought back the ideas of the Greek philosophers Plato and Aristotle. At the time, almost no one in Europe knew of these great thinkers.

▲ The Arabic calligraphy on this tile reads, "Allah is Great."

Art and Architecture

The caliphate is also known for its achievements in art and architecture. The caliphs built beautiful **mosques**, which are Muslim places of worship. Some large mosques feature grand domes, columns, and arches. Next to many mosques are tall **minarets**, towers from which Muslims are called to pray five times each day.

Traditional Muslim artists never showed animals or people in their work, because it is against Islamic law to create images of living things. Instead, artists created complex patterns called arabesques, and used calligraphy, or artistic handwriting, to decorate buildings. Muslim weavers made rugs with floral patterns that are still treasured today. Musicians performed on a pear-shaped string instrument called an *oud* and, later, an early guitar that is the ancestor of the instrument we use today.

QUICK CHECK

Summarize How did new ideas spread throughout the caliphate?

SCIENCE AND MEDICINE

▲ This painting of a pharmacy was used in a book of Avicenna's writings.

Some of the greatest Muslim achievements were in science and medicine. Muslim doctors started the world's first schools of pharmacy. There they discovered drugs still in use today. Doctors in the caliphate were the first to identify and treat diseases such as measles. In Baghdad, some doctors worked in large hospitals. Others traveled with nurses by camel, in "moving hospitals," to treat people outside the city for free.

Muslim scholars built on the ideas of ancient Greek mathematicians. They replaced Roman numerals with an ancient Indian system of numbers that included a zero. Known as Hindu-Arabic numerals, these are the numbers we use today. Muslim scholars also expanded the branch of mathematics they called *al-jabr*. We know it today as algebra.

Astronomy was important in the caliphate. Astronomers built observatories to study the skies so they could improve their calendar, which was based on the movement of the moon. To help sailors navigate, Muslim scholars improved the **astrolabe**, a device that helps calculate a ship's position on Earth. These advances helped them make more accurate maps.

PEOPLE

Muslim doctor and philosopher Ibn Sinah, also known as **Avicenna**, published a medical encyclopedia that taught how to treat various illnesses. The book was used in Europe and Africa for 600 years.

Avicenna

Ibn Batuta's Travels

A traveler named Ibn Batuta used some of these maps to undertake a 75,000-mile journey. In about 1325, the 22-year-old decided to fulfill his Muslim religious duty. He set out alone on a hajj to Makkah. He traveled by foot, boat, horse, and camel. After reaching Makkah, he continued traveling for the next 29 years. When he became ill on his journey, he told another traveler:

> If God decrees my death, then my death shall be on the road, with my face set towards [Makkah].
>
> —IBN BATUTA

By the end of his travels, he had journeyed nearly 75,000 miles from his home in present-day Morocco. He had crossed Africa, India, and Europe. Ibn Batuta may have seen more of the world than anyone alive at the time.

The Empire Breaks Apart

As the Muslim empire grew larger, it became harder to manage. Local rulers began refusing to follow the caliphs in Baghdad. By 973, Spain, Morocco, and Egypt had become independent caliphates, with local rulers.

The caliphs had hired Seljuk Turk soldiers from lands far north of Arabia. These warriors later converted to Islam. Eventually, the Seljuks began to build their own empire and fight against the caliphate. In the wars that followed, they conquered much of what is

today Iran and Turkey. Then, in 1055, they captured Baghdad and took control of the caliphate. They would rule it for 200 years.

The Seljuks defeated the Byzantine Empire in battle in 1071. Byzantine leaders turned to the Pope and other Western European leaders for help. The lengthy wars that followed would become known as the Crusades. The Crusades continued off and on for the next 200 years. These battles between the Christians of Western Europe and the Muslims of today's Middle East would cause great changes in Europe, Arabia, and Asia. You will read more about those wars in the next unit.

QUICK CHECK

Cause and Effect What was the effect of the Seljuk Turks' defeat of the Byzantine Empire?

Check Understanding

1. **VOCABULARY** Write a paragraph about the Muslim empire using these words.

   bazaar   mosque   astrolabe

2. **READING SKILL Summarize**
   Use the chart from page 140 to summarize the most important achievements of the Muslim empire.

 3. Write About It How did the Muslim empire change the places it conquered?

Lesson 3

VOCABULARY

sultan p. 149

divan p. 150

grand vizier p. 150

Janissaries p. 150

Grand Mufti p. 150

READING SKILL

Summarize

How did the Ottomans rule their empire?

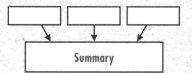

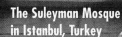

Summary

New York Academic Content Standards

2.1, 2.2, 2.3, 3.1, 3.2, 4.1

The Ottoman Empire

The Suleyman Mosque in Istanbul, Turkey

Visual Preview

How did diversity affect the Ottoman Empire?

A Turks united to form the Ottoman Empire and conquered Constantinople.

B The empire expanded into North Africa and eastern Europe.

C After the death of Suleyman the Magnificent, the empire declined.

Ⓐ DAWN OF A NEW EMPIRE

The Greeks called the Asian part of modern Turkey Anatolia, or "Rising Sun." In the 1400s, Muslims from this region conquered what remained of the Byzantine Empire. The sun had set on the Byzantines, and a new empire had risen to take their place.

The Anatolia region was part of the Eastern Roman Empire until it was conquered by Arab armies. It then became part of the Muslim Empire. Around 1300, a group of people from Central Asia, called the Ottoman Turks, came into the region and conquered Anatolia. The Ottoman Turks united under a **sultan**, or Muslim ruler, named Osman. In his honor, these Turks called themselves *Osmanli*, or Ottoman.

Conquest of Constantinople

By the middle of the 1400s, all that was left of the old Byzantine Empire was the city of Constantinople. The city posed a great challenge to any invaders It was surrounded by water on three sides and a high wall on the fourth. Still, in 1453 a 22-year-old Ottoman sultan named Mehmet II assembled a huge army and became determined to capture the city.

As he began his attack, Mehmet II ordered his soldiers to build a pair of forts on the Bosporus Strait to prevent ships with food, supplies, and soldiers from reaching Constantinople. Still, the defenders of the city fought hard and trusted in their city's thick walls.

EVENT

On April 22, 1453, people in Constantinople saw 70 enemy ships being dragged over land and pushed into the city's own harbor. **Mehmet's attack on Constantinople** was about to begin.

Mehmet II Conquers Constantinople

The Ottomans, however, had a new weapon—the cannon. These powerful guns pounded the walls of Constantinople day and night for over a month.

By 1453, the people of Constantinople were surrounded by the Ottoman army. With no way to get fresh supplies, they worked frantically to repair their city walls. But the last city of the Byzantine Empire had no chance. Mehmet II launched a brilliant naval attack, and Ottoman forces broke through the old Roman walls on May 29. Constantinople fell, and the city became the capital of Mehmet II's Ottoman Empire.

QUICK CHECK

Summarize How did Turkish troops conquer Constantinople?

The armies of the Ottoman Empire conquered much of eastern Europe and North Africa. To rule this large territory, the sultans formed a **divan**, or group of advisers, to help them make important decisions. The **grand vizier**, a chief adviser, met with foreign officials and carried out the sultans' decisions. The sultans also had special soldiers called **Janissaries**. These men were kidnapped as boys and trained to be loyal only to the sultan. They became very powerful soldiers, but sometimes they overthrew the sultans.

The Ottoman Empire was a Muslim empire, and a religious leader known as the **Grand Mufti** decided how to apply Islamic law to the daily life of its people. Like the caliphs before them, the Ottoman rulers were more tolerant of different religions and nationalities than European kings of the time. Christians and Jews paid higher taxes but were allowed to practice their religions freely.

Suleyman the Magnificent

The most famous Ottoman sultan was Suleyman the Magnificent, who led the empire to its greatest size by 1550. Under Suleyman, Constantinople again became a center for trade, and the wealth of the empire increased. The map on page 151 shows how Constantinople was well located to be a trade center. Coffee from Arabia; rice and gold from Egypt; furs from Russia; and cheese and wheat from the Black Sea region all flowed into Constantinople. The ancient Romans had once said, "All roads lead to Rome." During Suleyman's time, all roads led to Constantinople.

The city attracted people from around the world and had great ethnic diversity. The sultans welcomed Jews in their capital, where they worked alongside Greeks and Italians. In the next unit, you will read how Spain's rulers forced all the Jews in that country to leave in 1492.

Enslaved people could also find success in the Ottoman Empire. Government officials would visit towns throughout the empire each year to find non-Muslim boys who were at least 8 years old. The boys were sent to Constantinople to serve as slaves in the palace and to be educated. Many of these slaves became surgeons, military commanders, or architects.

▲ **Suleyman the Magnificent**

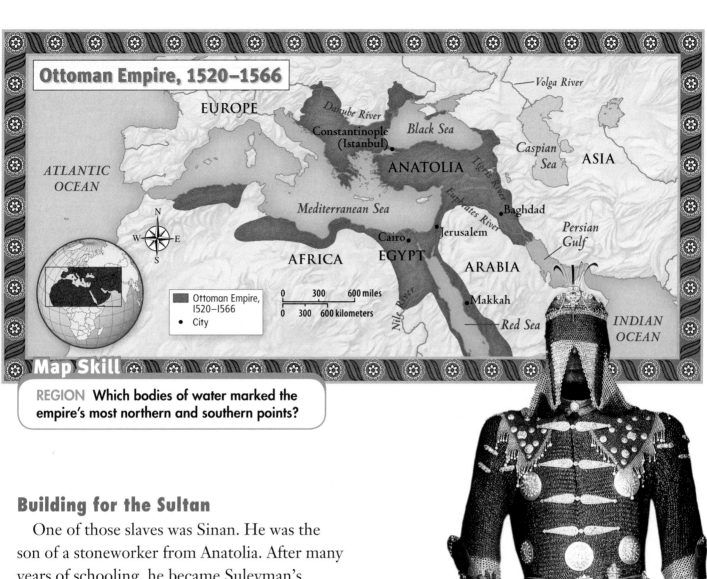

Ottoman Empire, 1520–1566

EUROPE

Volga River

Danube River

Constantinople
(Istanbul)

Black Sea

Caspian
Sea

ASIA

ATLANTIC
OCEAN

ANATOLIA

Tigris River

Mediterranean Sea

Euphrates River

Baghdad

Persian
Gulf

Cairo

Jerusalem

AFRICA

EGYPT

ARABIA

Nile River

Makkah

Red Sea

INDIAN
OCEAN

Ottoman Empire,
1520–1566
• City

0   300   600 miles
0   300   600 kilometers

N W E S

Map Skill

REGION Which bodies of water marked the empire's most northern and southern points?

Building for the Sultan

One of those slaves was Sinan. He was the son of a stoneworker from Anatolia. After many years of schooling, he became Suleyman's official architect. Sinan designed mosques, markets, libraries, and hospitals for the sultan. Sinan also designed buildings for Suleyman's wife, Hurrem Sultan. These included an orphanage and a soup kitchen for the poor. One of his greatest achievements was the Mosque of Suleyman, which can still be seen in Istanbul, the modern name of Constantinople. The soaring domes of the mosque influenced later European architects.

This suit of armor and shield belonged to the Ottoman Sultan Mustapha III (1717-1774) ▶

QUICK CHECK

Summarize What helped make Constantinople a center of trade?

THE EMPIRE WEAKENS

More than a century after Suleyman's time, in 1683, Ottoman armies attacked Vienna, Austria. At the start of the attack, the Ottoman general sent a message to the Austrian general, telling him that he planned to eat breakfast in Vienna the next day. Weeks passed, but Vienna did not fall. The Austrian general sent a message back to the Ottomans: "Your breakfast is getting cold!"

As people across Europe waited to see who would win the battle for Vienna, the king of Poland agreed to send troops to help support the city. With the help of the Poles, Austria fought off the Ottomans. No one realized it at the time, but this was the beginning of the end of the Ottoman Empire.

During the battle for Vienna, some Austrian bakers made a breakfast roll shaped like the crescent moon, the symbol of the Muslim Ottoman Empire. These rolls are known today as croissants. After the battle, when Austrian troops reached the abandoned tents of the Ottoman generals, they found ground beans. Europeans soon developed a taste for the drink made from those beans—coffee.

A view of present-day Istanbul ▶

"The Sick Man"

After the surprising failure of the Turks at Vienna, neighboring countries began to chip away at the Ottoman Empire. Russia seized territory north of the Black Sea. Austria conquered much of the area known as the Balkans. The sultans would hold on to power until World War I, but by the 1800s, the ruler of Russia had begun calling the empire, then limited to today's Turkey, "the sick man of Europe."

QUICK CHECK

Draw Conclusions Why did other countries begin to attack Ottoman lands after 1683?

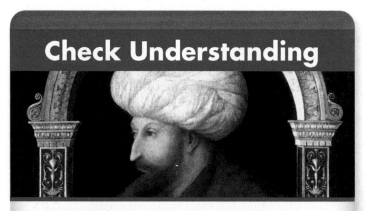

Check Understanding

1. **VOCABULARY** Describe a visit to Constantinople at the height of the Ottoman Empire, using these vocabulary words.

   sultan   **grand vizier**   **Janissaries**

2. **READING SKILL Summarize** 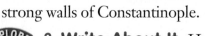 Use your chart from page 148 to show how the Ottomans dealt with the strong walls of Constantinople.

3. **Write About It** How did the Ottoman Empire change from the reign of Suleyman to the defeat at Vienna in 1683?

Chart and Graph Skills

Use Bar and Line Graphs

VOCABULARY

bar graph
line graph

The Ottoman Empire stretched from Constantinople into Europe, Asia, and Africa. Many Ottoman cities are still major cities in the region today. You can learn about them by studying graphs. Graphs are diagrams that present information. Two kinds of graphs are shown below. **Bar graphs** compare information at a specific point in time. **Line graphs** show changes over time.

Learn It

To find out what information a graph displays, look at its title. What does this bar graph show?

● Study the labels on the bar graph. The numbers on the left show how many millions of people live in each city today. The names of the cities are at the bottom.

● Now study the line graph. The red line shows how the number of people living in Istanbul changed over time.

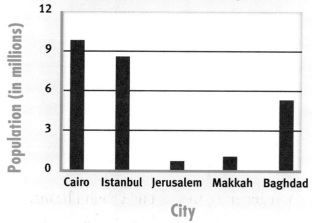

Try It

● Look at the bar graph. What cities have a smaller population than Istanbul?

● Now look at the line graph. During which period of time did Istanbul's population increase most? When did it decrease?

Apply It

● Draw a bar graph to show how many students are in each grade of your school.

● What kind of graph would you use to show how the number of students in your school has changed from year to year?

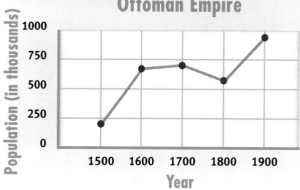

Lesson 4

VOCABULARY

sickle p. 158

textile p. 159

mint p. 161

READING SKILL

Summarize

Describe the rise and fall of the Kushites.

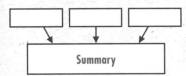

Summary

New York Academic Content Standards

2.1, 2.2, 2.3, 3.1, 3.2

Models of
Nubian archers

Visual Preview

How did outside cultures influence early African kingdoms?

A The kingdom of Nubia became wealthy from trade and often warred with Egypt.

B After the Kushites conquered Egypt, they began to follow Egyptian customs.

C Iron weapons and tools changed Kushite culture.

D Aksum was one of the world's first Christian kingdoms.

NUBIA

Egypt was not the only kingdom to rise along the banks of the Nile River. Thousands of years ago, another kingdom, Nubia, developed to the south of Egypt. Nubia's soil was not as fit for farming as Egypt's, but its people had other ways of gaining wealth. For one, they had gold.

Like Egypt, Nubia had upper and lower regions. Lower Nubia had rich farmland. The high stone cliffs of Upper Nubia to the south had natural resources including gold, iron, and copper. These made the kingdom wealthy.

▲ A Nubian scorpion pendant

Nubian Daily Life

We know some of Nubia's history from Egyptian writings. Since Egypt and Nubia were often enemies, however, historians think that Egyptian scribes may not have described Nubia fairly. Archaeologists have learned more about daily life in Nubia from excavations, or explorations, of ancient settlements.

Hunter-gatherers first settled in Nubia around 6000 B.C. They moved from place to place to hunt animals and gather wild plants. Their diet also included ostrich eggs. These people eventually settled in villages along the Nile.

By about 3500 B.C., Nubia was part of a trade route connecting Egypt with its rich gold mines. Nubian gold was shipped north to be made into beautiful objects

for Egypt's pharaohs. This gold, however, also attracted Egypt's armies. They invaded and by 1500 B.C., had taken control of the entire kingdom. Egypt and Nubia would remain united for about 400 years.

QUICK CHECK

Compare and Contrast **How were ancient Nubia and Egypt alike and different?**

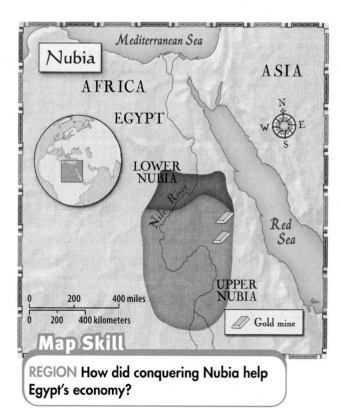

Map Skill

REGION **How did conquering Nubia help Egypt's economy?**

ⓑ THE KUSHITES

Around 850 B.C. Egyptian power declined, and they lost their grip on Nubia. Egypt and Nubia were no longer united. Egyptian armies returned to Egypt, but large parts of Egyptian culture remained. Nubians merged their old customs with their adopted Egyptian culture to create the new kingdom of Kush.

One of the strongest Kushite kings was Kashta, who ruled from about 806 to 750 B.C. Kashta invaded Egypt and even captured its capital city, Thebes. When his son, Piye, became king, he continued the conquest of Egypt.

Piye's armies were among the first to use elephants in battle. Kushite soldiers also had stronger weapons than their enemies and were feared around the region. By 728 B.C., King Piye had taken control of all of Egypt.

Male and Female Rulers

Royal Kushite women were often co-rulers with their husbands or sons. Some powerful women even ruled Kush on their own. They held the title *Kandake*, which meant queen, or mother of the prince. The modern name Candace comes from *Kandake*.

Kush and Nubia

Mediterranean Sea

ASIA

Memphis

AFRICA

EGYPT

Thebes

N W E S

Kush

Nubia

• City

Nile River

Napata

Meroë

Red Sea

0   200   400 miles
0 200 400 kilometers

Map Skill

MOVEMENT **About how many miles did Kushite troops travel from Napata to Thebes?**

After conquering Egypt, Kushite rulers brought Egyptian art, writing, and other customs back to their kingdom. They began to wrap their dead as mummies and to bury them in Egyptian-style coffins. They also built Egyptian-style temples and pyramids as burial sites. Many of the small pyramids they constructed can still be seen today in the nation of Sudan.

QUICK CHECK

Summarize How did Egyptian culture influence Kush?

More than 2,500 years after they were built, Kushite pyramids still stand in the deserts of Sudan. ▼

Citizenship

LEADERSHIP

In the kingdom of Kush, women could rule alongside their husbands or sons, or on their own. The idea that a woman could lead people as well as a man was unusual in the ancient world, but not today. The United States has not had a female president yet, but as of 2007 there were 17 women in the Senate. Although they disagree on many issues, they sometimes come together to speak out on issues that are important to women.

Write About It How do women and men work together as leaders in your community?

C THE POWER OF IRON

Kushite rulers did not control Egypt very long. Around 662 B.C., invaders from Assyria entered Egypt. You have already read about the power of Assyria's armies. Their weapons were made of iron. Kushite swords and shields were made of copper, which is softer than iron. They were no match for Assyria's heavier weapons. The Assyrians defeated the Kushite armies, who retreated south to their homeland.

However, Kush learned from its defeat. Back home, craftworkers learned how to make things from iron, too. Soon the Kushites had iron weapons themselves, as well as new iron

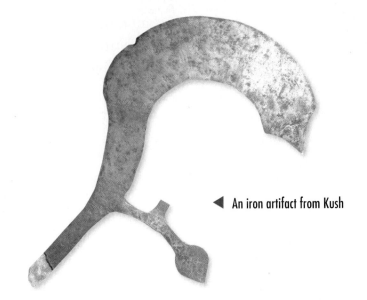

◀ An iron artifact from Kush

farming tools, such as plows, hoes, and sickles. A **sickle** is a tool with a curved blade used to cut grain and tall grass. With these new tools, Kushite farming improved and the kingdom's economy grew.

A carved ram protects the entrance to a Kushite temple. ▼

▲ This Egyptian wall painting shows Nubians carrying offerings to Egyptian rulers.

The Fall of Kush

Egyptian invaders attacked Kush in 593 B.C. and destroyed its capital, Napata. So Kush moved its capital to Meroë, farther south on the Nile River in present-day Ethiopia. Nearby iron mines had already made Meroë an important Kushite iron-working center.

Despite the battles with Egypt and Assyria, Kush remained a wealthy empire because of its trade routes to regions south of the Sahara Desert and to locations as far away as Rome, China, and India. Goods were sent from Meroë to the Red Sea to be shipped out along Indian Ocean trade routes. Kushite merchants traded valuable goods like leopard skins, ivory, and ebony wood. They also traded iron and **textiles**, or woven cloth.

In the A.D. 200s, a new trade route developed for shipping goods through the new kingdom of Aksum on the west coast of the Red Sea near Meroë, just southeast of Kush. Trade brought wealth and power to Aksum, and in 350, its armies captured and destroyed Meroë. After almost 3,000 years, the Nubian-Kushite civilization came to an end.

QUICK CHECK

Summarize Why was iron so important to the Kushites?

D AKSUM

By A.D. 350, Aksum was the most important kingdom in northeast Africa. Its location in the hills and mountains of present-day Ethiopia and Eritrea protected it from enemies. Its control of trade routes between the Nile Valley and the Red Sea made Aksum wealthy. As with other civilizations at the time, trade brought changes to Aksum society. Scholars and poets who followed the region's trade routes brought new ideas and religions to the kingdom.

The early people of Aksum worshipped many gods. Soon after Aksum conquered Kush, the kingdom was led by a boy king, Ezana. He had two close advisers, brothers who had come to Aksum as children with their uncle, a Christian merchant. One of the brothers taught Ezana about Christianity. In about 334, Ezana converted and made Christianity the official religion of his kingdom. Aksum was one of the world's earliest Christian nations. Today, about half of all Ethiopians are Christians.

▼ Seen from above, the stone churches of Aksum look like Christian crosses.

▲ Under King Lalibela, Aksum carved large stone churches from single pieces of stone. The churches still stand in Ethiopia today.

Aksum minted coins like these out of gold. But when the kingdom weakened, it began making coins of bronze. After Aksum lost its trade routes to the caliphate, it stopped minting coins altogether.

Golden Coins

Ezana opened up new trade routes with India and the Roman Empire during his reign, making Aksum wealthy and powerful. At this time, Aksum became the first African kingdom to **mint** its own coins. To mint is to make coins. Aksum's coins were made of gold, and most were stamped with pictures of Aksum's kings. After Ezana converted to Christianity, he ordered the Christian cross added to Aksum's coins.

The Fall of Aksum

By 700, the Muslim caliphate to the north had seized control of Aksum's shipping routes on the Red Sea and beyond. As the kingdom's wealth declined, it stopped minting coins and moved its capital from the city of Aksum to a southern farming region, Kubar. Soon after the capital moved, a group of Aksum nobles called the Zagwe overthrew Aksum's rulers.

Churches of Rock

Like the earlier leaders of Aksum, the Zagwe were Christian. The most powerful Zagwe king was Lalibela, who ruled from 1185 to 1225. His kingdom, Ethiopia, had a capital named Lalibela in his honor. He ordered workers to carve 11 stone churches in his capital city. Many of these churches were carved from huge blocks of stone—one block per church. Skilled workers were brought in from as far away as Egypt for this project.

Visitors to Ethiopia can still see these churches today. Christian services take place at the sites of some of the churches, following traditions that developed under the Zagwe rulers.

QUICK CHECK

Summarize How did Aksum's culture change when Ezana became king?

Check Understanding

1. **VOCABULARY** Use the following vocabulary to describe the economy of early African kingdoms.

   sickle   textile   mint

2. **READING SKILL Summarize** Use the chart from page 154 to describe the rise of the Kushite kingdom.

 3. **Write About It** How did outside cultures influence early African kingdoms?

WEST AFRICAN EMPIRES

The Great Mosque in Djenne, Mali, is the world's largest adobe building.

Visual Preview

How did trade affect the kingdoms of Ghana, Mali, and Songhai?

A The gold trade in West Africa led to the rise of wealthy empires.

B Ghana's large army helped it control the gold trade.

C Rulers like Mansa Musa made Mali a religious and cultural center.

D The Yoruba ruled its territory for centuries, until it fell to Great Britain.

A TRADE IN WEST AFRICA

Around A.D. 700, North African traders began traveling in caravans south across the Sahara Desert. The journey over the hot sands was long and difficult. Why would these traders brave the desert to get to the cities of West Africa? Gold!

Around 400 B.C., the Berbers, a group of herders, settled in what are today the North African countries of Morocco, Algeria, and Tunisia. For hundreds of years, the Berbers crossed the Sahara Desert to trade with people in West Africa. The region southwest of the Sahara was a land of gold and great wealth. Traders were willing to risk the dangers of crossing the desert to trade in West Africa.

Trade Routes

Later, the Berbers learned to use camels to cross the desert. Camels helped them travel faster and farther. The animals can walk about 18 miles a day and carry close to 300 pounds on their backs. They have large, wide feet good for walking on sand, and they can travel up to 10 days without drinking water. Some Berber caravans heading to West Africa had hundreds of men and camels. They carried valuable goods and money. West African cities taxed these traders as they passed through. These taxes helped cities on trade routes grow in wealth and power.

Rivers helped West African cities grow, too. The major cities of Gao, Tombouctou, and Djenne developed along the Niger River. Trade routes linked them to cities in North Africa. Other African trade routes stretched west to the Atlantic Ocean, north to the Mediterranean Sea, and east to the Arabian Peninsula.

QUICK CHECK

Summarize How did camels help trade between North and West Africa?

Around A.D. 400 the empire of Ghana came to power in West Africa. Its location near trade routes helped it gain wealth and power. Ancient Ghana contained parts of the present-day countries of Mali and Mauritania. The modern nation of Ghana, which takes its name from the ancient empire, is located south of this area. At its peak, in the year 1000, ancient Ghana covered more than 250,000 square miles—an area about the size of Texas.

Building an Army

Ghana's kings grew wealthy collecting taxes from traders. These taxes supported the royal family and paid for an army to guard Ghana's trade routes. The army became the strongest in West Africa, with as many as 200,000 skilled soldiers armed with weapons like iron-tipped spears and arrows. These weapons were stronger than the metals used by other armies in the region. Ghana's army used its advantages to conquer neighboring villages and seize the region's gold mines for its kings.

Gold for Salt

Ghana's kings controlled gold production in the empire. This way, they could decide how much gold could be sold at any time. As you will read in the Primary Sources box on the next page, the kingdom's rulers required that all gold nuggets would be kept by the kingdom, but they allowed visiting traders to trade for gold dust.

The control of Ghana's gold trade is an example of the economic rule of supply and demand. The supply of a resource, good, or product is the amount available for sale or trade. Demand is the number of people who want to purchase or trade for the product or service. According to supply and demand, items that are available in large amounts should have a low price, but rare items should be more expensive. By limiting the amount of gold available for trade, Ghana's kings kept the demand for gold—and its price—at a high level.

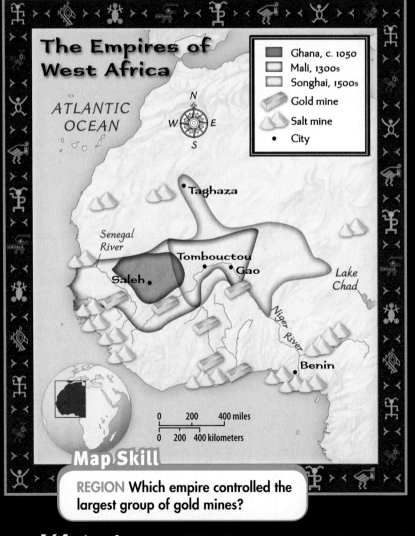

The Empires of West Africa

- Ghana, c. 1050
- Mali, 1300s
- Songhai, 1500s
- Gold mine
- Salt mine
- • City

ATLANTIC OCEAN

N W E S

Taghaza

Senegal River

Tombouctou
Gao

Saleh

Lake Chad

Niger River

Benin

0   200   400 miles
0   200   400 kilometers

Map Skill

REGION Which empire controlled the largest group of gold mines?

A brass weight (left) was used to weigh gold nuggets (center), which were kept in boxes like the one at the right.

Many merchants in West Africa traded their gold for salt. At the time, salt was the second-most valuable trade good in Africa. It was needed to flavor and preserve food in the hot climate. Salt was so valuable, in fact, that some cultures made their coins from it. West African merchants traded gold for blocks of salt carried to the region from North Africa by the Berbers. The Berbers then took the gold north to Europe, where it sold for a high price.

The End of Ghana's Empire

Ghana's kings controlled the gold trade for more than 500 years. In that time, new gold mines were discovered outside of the empire. As other groups began selling gold, Ghana's wealth and power declined. In 1075, Berbers invaded Ghana and weakened the empire's rulers even more. By 1240, Ghana had collapsed, and a new West African empire called Mali had emerged.

Primary Sources

A Muslim geographer named al-Bakri explained how the Ghana kings controlled the gold trade:

"All pieces of gold that are found in this empire belong to the king of Ghana, but he leaves to his people the gold-dust. . . . Without this precaution, gold would become so plentiful that it would practically lose its value."

From *The Book of Routes and Realms*

Write About It Why was it a good idea for Ghana's rulers to let the people keep the kingdom's gold dust?

QUICK CHECK

Cause and Effect **How did Ghana control the price of gold?**

C MALI AND SONGHAI

The empire of Mali emerged in the same region of Africa as Ghana, but it grew much larger. Mali extended east to the Niger River and west to the Atlantic Ocean. Like Ghana, it grew rich controlling the region's gold trade. Sundiata, the empire's first great ruler, came to power in 1230. He quickly expanded Mali's control of West African trade routes.

Sundiata of Mali

Tales of Sundiata's life have been told in West Africa for centuries. Local storytellers called **griots** would memorize the stories and retell them to the next generation. Sundiata's story begins with the death of Mali's first king. The old man had chosen one son, Sumaguru, from among all his children to follow him as king. Soon after he became king, Sumaguru killed all of his brothers to get rid of any rivals to the throne. He did, however, let one brother live—Sundiata. The boy was unable to walk, so Sumaguru thought Sundiata was harmless. It was a serious mistake.

Sumaguru was a cruel leader, and people throughout the kingdom called for someone to save them from his brutal rule. Sundiata decided that it was his duty to save Mali from his brother. He forced himself to stand up and to walk. As stories of his courage spread, people began to call him the "Lion Prince." Sundiata defeated his brother and became king of Mali in 1230.

Mansa Musa

Mali reached its greatest power in the early 1300s. From 1312 to 1337, Mansa Musa, a strong ruler related to Sundiata, expanded Mali's borders and gained control of more gold mines. In Mansa Musa's time, Mali was the source of half of all the gold traded in the world.

Mansa Musa used the empire's wealth to build schools, libraries, and universities in major cities like Tombouctou (Timbuktu), Djenne, and Niani. Tombouctou was Mali's cultural center and attracted scholars from across the Islamic world.

This map of west Africa from 1375 shows Mansa Musa in Mali, holding a gold nugget. ▼

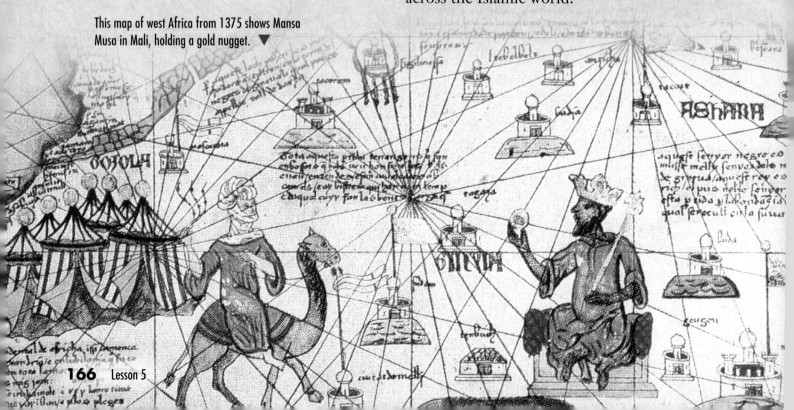

▲ This horse and rider from West Africa is made of terra cotta.

Mansa Musa was a devout Muslim. Under his rule, many people in the Mali Empire converted to Islam. He ordered mosques built across the empire. In 1324 Mansa Musa led hundreds of people on a hajj, or pilgrimage, to Makkah. As they traveled, they gave away tons of gold. In fact, they handed out so much gold to people in Egypt that the price of gold there dropped for 10 years.

The Songhai Empire

Around the time Christopher Columbus sailed to the Americas, Mali's kings lost control of West Africa's gold-for-salt trade, and a new empire took control of the valuable trade routes. This was Songhai, and it soon controlled more territory in West Africa than Mali ever had.

The founder of the Songhai Empire was Sunni Ali. In 1464 his troops conquered Tombouctou and took over most of the Niger River valley. When Sunni Ali died in 1492, the kingdom was seized by a soldier named Askia Muhammad. His army was the first in the region to be paid a regular wage. Soon after Askia's death, civil war weakened the empire. As Songhai struggled to find unity, invaders from Morocco crushed its army in 1591 and ended the empire.

QUICK CHECK

Cause and Effect How did Mansa Musa's religious beliefs affect his empire?

DataGraphic

The Gold and Salt Trade

Ghana and Mali were rich in gold but needed to trade with North African peoples for other important resources. Read the quote and look at the chart below. Answer the questions.

❝The merchants. . . place their wares on the ground and then depart, and so the people of [Ghana] come, bearing gold which they leave beside the merchandise and then depart. The [merchants] then return, and if they are satisfied with what they have found, they take it. If not, they go away again, and the people return and add to the price.❞

—Masudi, an Arab traveler, writing around A.D. 950

African Trade

From North Africa	From West Africa
Salt	Gold
Metal goods	Kola nuts
Swords	Farm produce
Horses	
Cloth	

Think About Trade Based on the table, what can you say about the natural resources of West Africa?

▲ A wooden Yoruba screen

Like other West African empires, the Yoruba passed on stories of their gods and rulers through griots. Historians have learned a lot about Yoruba history from these oral histories. Today, the Yoruba culture can be found in the nation of Nigeria. Between 1600 and 1800, many Yoruba people were enslaved and sent to North and South America. As a result, elements of Yoruba culture can also be found in Brazil, Cuba, and the United States.

QUICK CHECK

Compare and Contrast How was the fall of the Yoruba Empire different from the declines of earlier empires in the region?

The Yoruba were among the last groups to control the wealthy West African region. The Yoruba ruled the area around present-day Nigeria from the 1300s until the late 1800s. At that time, Great Britain conquered them and made the Yoruba territory a British colony. The British controlled the region until 1960.

Yoruba Culture

According to Yoruba stories, the first ruler of their capital city, Ife, was a religious leader named Oduduwa. In Ife, metalworkers used copper, bronze, and iron to create beautiful statues of their gods and rulers. Today, these statues can be found in museums around the world. Dancing and music were also important parts of Yoruba culture. The Yoruba danced as a part of their religious worship.

Check Understanding

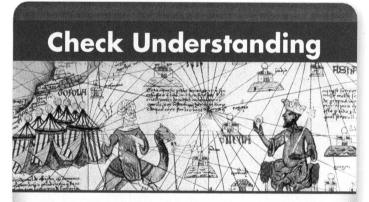

1. **VOCABULARY** Summarize this lesson using the following terms.

   supply   demand   griot

2. **READING SKILL Summarize** Use the chart from page 162 to tell how the gold trade affected the kingdoms of West Africa.

 3. **Write About It** What features did the empires of West Africa share?

Map and Globe Skills

Use Resource Distribution Maps

VOCABULARY

resource distribution map

The map below is a **resource distribution map**. This kind of map shows where natural resources are located in a region. The symbols on the map stand for specific resources. By studying the symbols, you can see where West Africans could find the resources they needed.

Learn It

- Read the map title. The map is titled, "Resource Distribution in West Africa, 1300s." It shows which natural resources were important in West Africa during this time.

- Study the map key. It identifies the symbols used for the resources shown on the map.

- Next, look at the map. The green area identifies Mali, the most powerful empire in the region at the time.

Try It

Use the map to answer these questions.

- Where could West Africans find salt?

- Which resources were available to people in the Mail Empire?

Apply It

- How could a resource distribution map of the region be different today?

- Why did kingdoms in the region trade gold for salt?

Resource Distribution in West Africa, 1300s

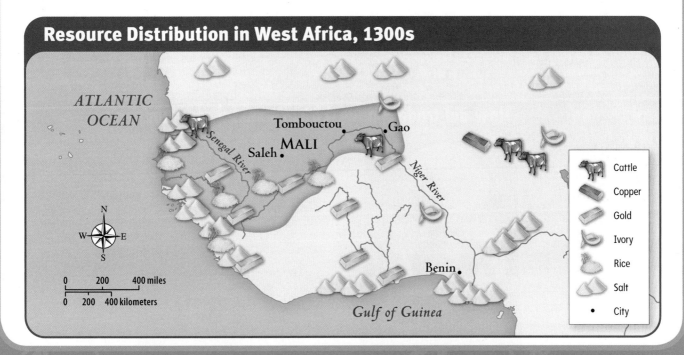

169

GREAT ZIMBABWE

Lesson 6

VOCABULARY

granary p. 171

dhow p. 173

READING SKILL

Summarize

How is the influence of Swahili trade settlements felt in East Africa today?

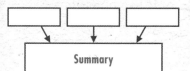

Summary

New York Academic Content Standards

2.1, 2.2, 2.3, 3.1, 3.2, 4.1

Some ruins of Great Zimbabwe still stand in Zimbabwe today.

Visual Preview

How did trade change African coastal communities?

A Great Zimbabwe became wealthy trading gold and ivory.

B East African coastal cities grew as trade with Asia increased.

GREAT ZIMBABWE

The workers heated the large rocks before breaking them into small bricks, then stacked the gray bricks to build high walls. In the middle of green fields and towering trees, they were creating a great city. There was much building yet to be done inside the walls. Zimbabwe was growing.

Between the Zambezi and Limpopo Rivers in southeastern Africa, in what are today the countries of Zimbabwe and Mozambique, a community began to develop around A.D. 1000. This was Great Zimbabwe. The people of Great Zimbabwe were called the Shona.

Great Zimbabwe had rich soil, fields for grazing, and trees for firewood. The Shona became wealthy and built an empire, however, by trading gold and ivory with merchants from as far away as Asia. By the 1500s, they had formed one of the largest and wealthiest empires in southern Africa.

A City of Stone

We do not know what the Shona called their empire. In their language, "Zimbabwe" means "stone house." The cities of Great Zimbabwe were built from huge granite stones. Other cultures in the region built similar houses, but none were as large as the Shona's. Their workers could build rock walls more than 30 feet high and 800 feet long. The weight of the

▲ A figure carved in Great Zimbabwe

huge granite rocks kept the walls in place. Many of the buildings still stand today.

Within these high walls, the Shona built stone houses and **granaries**, or towers to store their grain harvests. They also had advanced drainage systems, similar to modern sewers. Archaeologists have found more than 200 stone cities spread across Great Zimbabwe. There were probably about 10,000 people in the empire at its height. We do not know much about them or why their empire fell. The Shona did not leave oral or written records.

Their high stone walls may have been meant to protect their cities from enemy attacks. They may have been built to give privacy to Great Zimbabwe's leaders, or simply as a sign of their power. Archaeologists hope to discover whether famine, natural disaster, or some other cause led to Great Zimbabwe's decline.

QUICK CHECK

Summarize Why were strong walls important to the Shona?

171

B COASTAL TRADE

How did Shona traders in southeastern Africa get their products to the markets of Asia? They sold their goods to merchants in cities on Africa's northeastern coast. These merchants then took the goods to Asia by boat.

Swahili Merchants

Many of the traders in the coastal cities were Muslims who originally came from the Arabian Peninsula. These people came to be called "Swahili," from the African word meaning

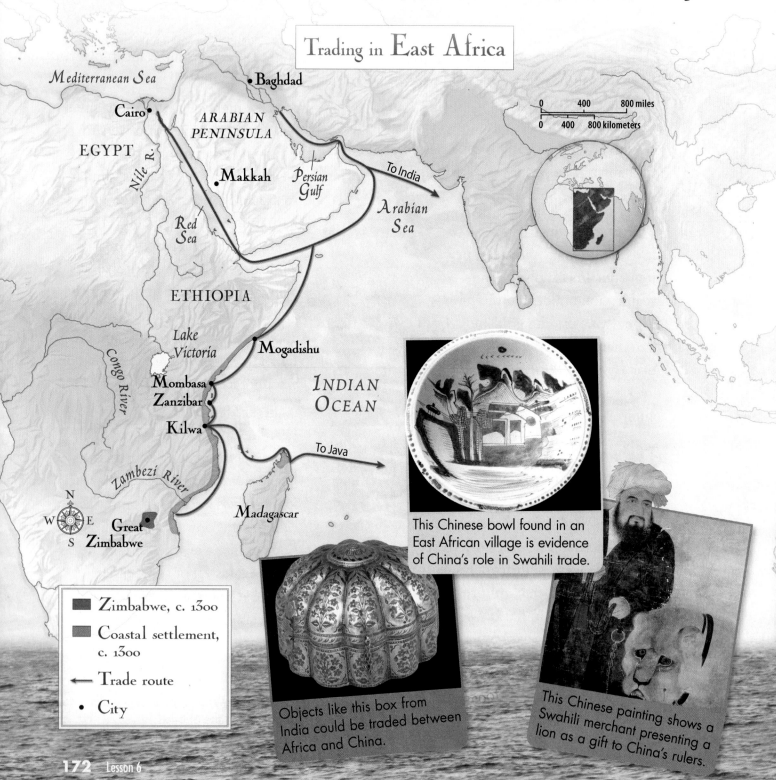

Trading in East Africa

Mediterranean Sea

• Baghdad

Cairo •

ARABIAN PENINSULA

EGYPT

Nile R.

• Makkah

Persian Gulf

To India

Red Sea

Arabian Sea

0   400   800 miles
0   400   800 kilometers

ETHIOPIA

Lake Victoria

• Mogadishu

INDIAN OCEAN

Congo River

Mombasa
Zanzibar

Kilwa

To Java

Zambezi River

Madagascar

N
W   E
S

Great Zimbabwe

This Chinese bowl found in an East African village is evidence of China's role in Swahili trade.

Objects like this box from India could be traded between Africa and China.

This Chinese painting shows a Swahili merchant presenting a lion as a gift to China's rulers.

■ Zimbabwe, c. 1300
■ Coastal settlement, c. 1300
← Trade route
• City

"people of the coast." Swahili merchants lived as far north as Mogadishu, in today's Somalia, and as far south as present-day Mozambique. Between 1000 and 1500, Swahili settlements gained control of the coastal trade routes and increased their wealth and influence in the region.

The largest Swahili cities and trading centers were Mogadishu and Zanzibar, which is on an island near present-day Tanzania. Sailors kept their boats in the safe harbor of Zanzibar. Around this time, Arab traders invented a large triangular sail for their small boats. These boats, which they called **dhows**, sailed up and down the east coast of Africa. As they were built larger and as sails improved, dhows could sail all the way to China. Dhows are still used by coastal traders in the region today.

Each Swahili city had a ruler who controlled its government and economy. The rulers of Mogadishu, for example, controlled much of East Africa's gold trade for more than 300 years. As Swahili cities grew in importance, the language of their rulers, also called Swahili, became the common language of people throughout eastern Africa.

A Variety of Goods

Swahili traders carried red, silver, and blue cloth, animal skins, metals, and jewels. When European traders arrived at Africa's east coast to trade with the Swahili, they discovered the great natural resources of the region. Soon, groups of European merchants and traders began to settle on the coast. Some set up colonies. By the 1800s, many of the Swahili settlements were under European control.

QUICK CHECK

Summarize How did technology affect the growth of trade in coastal Africa?

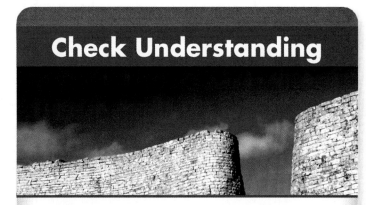

Check Understanding

1. **VOCABULARY** Write a postcard from Great Zimbabwe using these vocabulary terms.

   granary   dhow

2. **READING STRATEGY**
   Summarize Use the chart on page 168 to describe how the influence of Swahili trade settlements is felt in the region today.

   Summary

3. **Write About It** How did trade bring African, European, and Asian communities together?

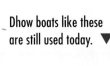

Dhow boats like these are still used today. ▼

173

Unit 3 Review and Assess

Vocabulary

Write the word from the list that best completes each sentence.

caliph   caravan   divan

minaret   pilgrimage

1. A _____ of 40 camels left today.

2. The call to prayer went out from the _____.

3. The _____ advised the sultan to attack the rebels.

4. They went on a ____to Makkah.

5. The _____ was a "successor" to Muhammad.

Comprehension and Critical Thinking

6. Why were caravans important to early Arabian civilizations?

7. Why was Kush able to conquer Egypt?

8. **Reading Skill** Why was iron important to Kush?

9. **Critical Thinking** How could an Arab have traded with Egyptians across the Red Sea?

10. **Critical Thinking** How do we know about events that took place in West Africa long ago?

Skill

Use Resource Distribution Maps

Write a complete sentence to answer each question.

11. What could traders from Benin offer in exchange for the resources they needed?

12. What would be the major resources on a resource distribution map of the area where you live today?

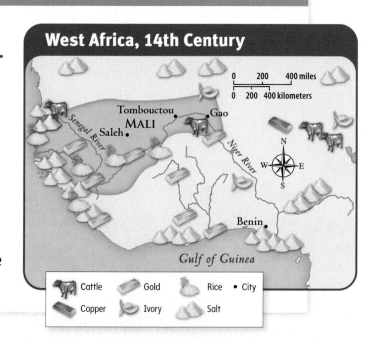

West Africa, 14th Century

Tombouctou Gao MALI Saleh Senegal River Niger River Benin Gulf of Guinea

N W E S

0 200 400 miles
0 200 400 kilometers

Cattle   Gold   Rice   • City
Copper   Ivory   Salt

New York English Language Arts Test Preparation

Directions

Read this quote. Then answer questions 1 and 2.

"In the name of Allah, the compassionate, the merciful, this is what [Arab military commander] Khalid ibn al-Walid would grant to the inhabitants of Damascus. . . . He promises to give them security for their lives, property and churches. Their city wall shall not be demolished, neither shall any Muslim be quartered [live] in their houses. Thereunto we give to them the pact of Allah and the protection of his Prophet, the Caliphs and the believers. So long as they pay the tax, nothing but good shall befall them."

-Khalid ibn al-Walid, during the Arab conquest

---

1 Who promised to spare Damascus?

  A Allah

  B Khalid ibn al-Walid

  C the Caliphs

  D the Muslims

2 What must the inhabitants of Damascus do to protect their lives, their city, and their churches?

  A attend church

  B join the Arab army

  C promise not to leave their homes

  D pay a tax

How do cultures influence each other?

Write About the Big Idea

Narrative Essay
In Unit 3, you read about how cultures influence each other. Review your notes in the completed foldable, and then use them to write an essay about the Big Idea.

Begin with an introductory paragraph, stating cultures' influence on each other.

Then write a paragraph or more describing how each civilization influenced, or was influenced by, other cultures.

Your final paragraph should summarize your main ideas.

The Arab Empire
The Ottoman Empire
East African Empires
African Trading Empires

Write a Travelog

Work independently to prepare a travelog, which is a piece of writing about a journey. The subject will be "A World of Influences." Here's how to make your travelog:

1. Choose two or more of the civilizations you read about in Unit 3, and describe how they came into contact with each other.

2. Write a fictional travelog from the viewpoint of someone from one of the civilizations who has traveled to a different civilization.

3. Include details about the influences the traveler sees.

4. If you like, illustrate your travelog with drawings or a collage. Share your travelog with your class.

Reference Section

The Reference Section has many parts, each with a different type of information. Use this section to look up people, places, and events as you study.

Cause and Effect

A cause is an action or event that makes something else happen. An effect is the result of the cause. When one event causes another event to happen, the events have a cause-and-effect relationship. Finding causes and effects will help you understand what you read in social studies.

Learn It

- As you read, ask yourself, "What happened?" The answer to this question helps you identify an effect.

- Then ask yourself, "Why did this happen?" Knowing why something happened will help you find its cause.

- Look for these clue words: *because*, *therefore*, *so*, and *as a result*. The clue words point out cause-and-effect relationships.

- Now read the passage below. Look for causes and effects.

A HISTORIC DISCOVERY

Cause
A landowner and his daughter wanted to take a walk.

Effect
They came across a cave entrance.

One day in 1879, a Spanish landowner and his daughter wanted to take a walk. They decided to walk in the fields near their village. They came across a cave entrance. The opening was narrow, so only the girl could squeeze inside. The girl looked up and gasped. She saw wonderful pictures of wild animals in orange, red, yellow, and black on the ceiling. Later explorers found similar paintings in caves in France. The little girl didn't know it, but she had discovered some of the oldest pictures in the world!

Try It

Copy the cause-and-effect chart below. Then fill in the chart with causes and effects from the paragraphs on page R2.

Cause	→	Effect
	→	
	→	
	→	

The cave entrance was small. What was the effect of this?

Apply It

Review the steps for understanding cause and effect on the previous page. Read these paragraphs. Then make a chart that lists three causes and three effects from the paragraphs.

The Spanish landowner found ancient bones and tools in the cave, so he said the paintings were also ancient. However, archaeologists said ancient people of this time could not have created such beautiful pictures.

The experts said the paintings were fake because they were too well-preserved. A few years later, similar paintings were found in a cave in France. The discovery of more caves with similar paintings led experts to believe that the paintings were genuine.

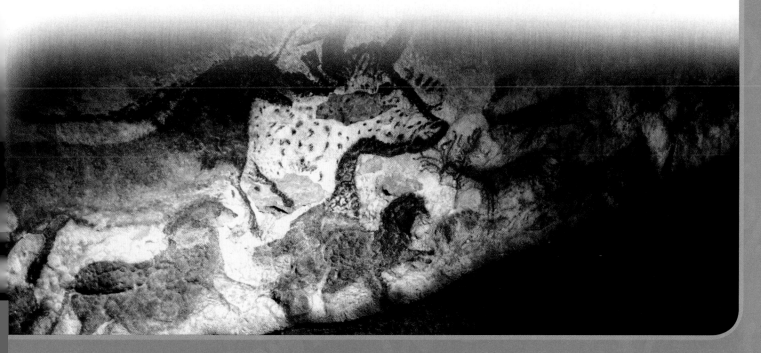

Unit 2 • Reading Skills

Fact and Opinion

A fact is a statement that can be proven to be true. A statement that expresses feelings or personal ideas about a subject is an opinion. A social studies textbook contains facts, such as dates, names, and places. A textbook can also include opinions, such as quotations from historians or eyewitnesses.

Learn It

Read the passage below about the Roman leader, Julius Caesar. Then follow the steps after the passage to identify facts and opinions in the excerpt.

Opinion
This is an opinion. There is no way to prove this statement.

Fact
This statement can be checked in reference sources.

"He was highly skilled in arms and horsemanship, and of incredible powers of endurance. On the march he headed his army, sometimes on horseback, but oftener on foot, bareheaded both in the heat of the sun and in rain. He covered great distances with incredible speed, making a hundred miles a day in a hired carriage and with little baggage, swimming the rivers which barred his path or crossing them on inflated skins, and very often arriving before the messengers sent to announce his coming."

SOURCE: *The Lives of the Twelve Caesars* by C. Suetonius Tranquillus

- Facts can be proven true. It is a fact that "he headed his army, sometimes on horseback, but oftener on foot."

- Opinions often contain value words, such as *incredible, I think, I feel, probably, perhaps,* and *maybe.*

Try It

Copy the chart below. Fill in the boxes with facts and opinions from the paragraph.

Fact	Opinion

Based on the facts in the paragraph, what is your opinion of Julius Caesar?

Apply It

Read a local newspaper. Find an example of a fact and an example of an opinion in the newspaper. Copy the sentences and write a paragraph explaining why you think each sentence is a fact or an opinion.

● What parts of the newspaper are most likely to contain opinions? Which parts are most likely to contain facts?

R5

Summarize

When you summarize, you retell briefly the main ideas of a passage. A summary is shorter than the original passage. A summary includes only important supporting details. You can use your summaries to review for a test.

Learn It

● Before writing a summary, identify the main ideas. Restate them simply.

● Include important details to support the main ideas.

● You should be able to summarize a paragraph in one or two sentences.

Read the passage below. Look for main ideas to include in a summary.

Main Idea
This is a main idea. Use it to begin your summary.

Africa had many ancient kingdoms. The wealth and power of kingdoms in West Africa made them famous in Europe and southwest Asia. The wealth of these kingdoms came from trade and gold mines. They also had powerful armies and well organized governments.

Details
These details support the main idea. Include them in your summary.

Today, there are echoes of the kingdoms in modern Africa. The West African nation of Ghana is named for one of the earliest African empires. Another African nation, Mali, uses the name of a later and even more powerful kingdom. There is also an African nation called Benin. It is named for a third powerful West African kingdom from ancient times.

Try It

Copy the summary chart below. Fill in the boxes to summarize the paragraphs on page R6.

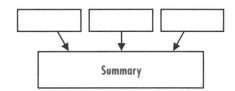

Summary

Write a summary of the paragraphs on page R6.

Apply It

- Review the steps for summarizing.
- Create a summary chart like the one on this page.
- Read the paragraph about Great Zimbabwe below.
- Use your chart to summarize the paragraph.

You may not realize that the modern nation of Zimbabwe takes its name from African history. Historians do not know as much about Great Zimbabwe as they do about some other African nations because there are few written records. Archaeologists have studied ruins and dug up artifacts. We do know that Great Zimbabwe grew rich on trade with cities on Africa's east coast.

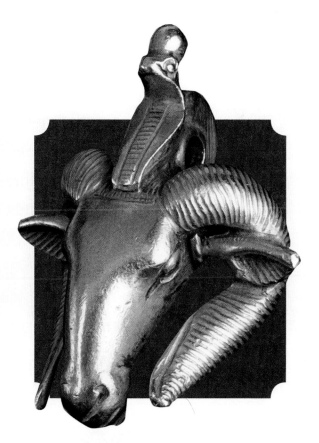

Geography Handbook

Geography and You

Geography is the study of many exciting things about our Earth and all of us who live here. Most people think of geography as learning about cities, states, and countries, but geography is more than that. Geography includes learning about bodies of water, such as oceans, lakes, and rivers. Geography also helps us learn about land, such as plains, mountains, and even volcanoes. Geography also helps people learn how to use land and water wisely.

People are part of geography, too. Geography includes the study of how people adapt to a new place in order to live there. How people move goods is also part of geography.

In fact, geography includes so many things that geographers have divided this information into six elements, or ideas, so you can better understand them.

Six Elements of Geography

The World in Spatial Terms: Where is a place located, and what land or water features does this place have?

Place and Region: What is special about a place, and what makes it different from other places?

Physical Systems: What has shaped the land and climate of a place, and how does this affect the plants, animals, and people there?

Human Systems: How do people, ideas, and goods move from place to place?

Environment and Society: How have people changed the land and water of a place, and how have the land and water affected the people of a place?

Uses of Geography: How does geography influence events of the past, present, and the future?

Five Themes of Geography

To understand how our world is connected, some geographers have broken down the study of geography into five different themes. The themes are **location**, **place**, **region**, **movement**, and **human interaction**. Understanding these themes will help you make sense of historical events.

1. Location

Eiffel Tower in Paris, France

Location means an exact spot on the planet. A location can be defined in several ways. Usually it includes a street name and number. You write a location when you address a letter. Location can also be a set of numbers. These numbers relate to a geographical grid system called longitude and latitude. This imaginary grid helps geographers find locations on Earth that do not have street numbers.

2. Place

Patagonia in Argentina

The description of a *place* is a combination of human and physical characteristics that make a place unique. To name a place, you would describe physical features, such as rivers, mountains, or valleys. You would also describe human characteristics of a place. This includes its population density, its major cities, or its language and religion.

3. Region

The Sahara in Algeria

A *region* is bigger than a place or a location. Regions cover large areas of land that share physical or human characteristics. For example, the nations of the Sahara have a hot, dry climate and populations that are centered near water. Other areas might be grouped because of cultural similarities. For example, many people of the Middle East share the religion of Islam.

4. Movement

Boats on the Grand Canal, China

Throughout history, there have been economic or political reasons for large numbers of people to *move* from one place to another. As people moved, they made changes, such as roads or canals. Cultures were often changed by encountering other cultures. Geographers look at why movements occur and how they affect cultures and environments.

5. Human Interaction

A wind farm in California

Geographers are interested in how the environment influences people. For example, people in cold areas need more fuel to generate heat in the winters. Geographers study how people adapt and change their environments. This *interaction* can determine how land is used for business, recreation, housing, and industry.

Dictionary of Geographic Terms

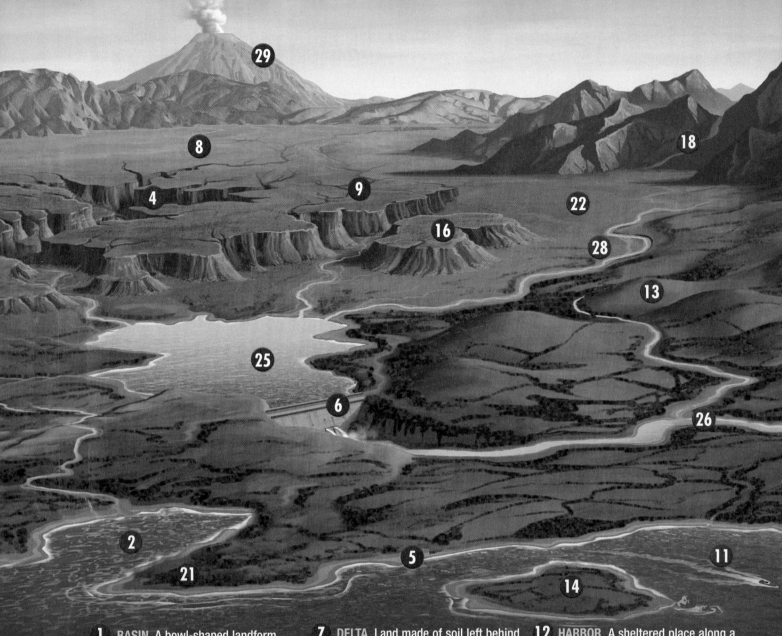

1 **BASIN** A bowl-shaped landform surrounded by higher land

2 **BAY** Part of an ocean or lake that extends deeply into the land

3 **CANAL** A channel built to carry water for irrigation or transportation

4 **CANYON** A deep, narrow valley with steep sides

5 **COAST** The land along an ocean

6 **DAM** A wall built across a river, creating a lake that stores water

7 **DELTA** Land made of soil left behind as a river drains into a larger body of water

8 **DESERT** A dry environment with few plants and animals

9 **FAULT** The border between two of the plates that make up Earth's crust

10 **GLACIER** A huge sheet of ice that moves slowly across the land

11 **GULF** Part of an ocean that extends into the land; larger than a bay

12 **HARBOR** A sheltered place along a coast where boats dock safely

13 **HILL** A rounded, raised landform; not as high as a mountain

14 **ISLAND** A body of land completely surrounded by water

15 **LAKE** A body of water completely surrounded by land

16 **MESA** A hill with a flat top; smaller than a plateau

17 **MOUNTAIN** A high landform with steep sides; higher than a hill

18 **MOUNTAIN PASS** A narrow gap through a mountain range

19 **MOUTH** The place where a river empties into a larger body of water

20 **OCEAN** A large body of salt water; oceans cover much of Earth's surface

21 **PENINSULA** A body of land nearly surrounded by water

22 **PLAIN** A large area of nearly flat land

23 **PLATEAU** A high, flat area that rises steeply above the surrounding land

24 **PORT** A place where ships load and unload their goods

25 **RESERVOIR** A natural or artificial lake used to store water

26 **RIVER** A stream of water that flows across the land and empties into another body of water

27 **SOURCE** The starting point of a river

28 **VALLEY** An area of low land between hills or mountains

29 **VOLCANO** An opening in Earth's surface through which hot rock and ash are forced out

30 **WATERFALL** A flow of water falling vertically

Reviewing Geography Skills

Read a Map

Most maps include standard features that help you understand the information on the map. One of the most important pieces of information you can get from a map is direction. The main directions are north, south, east, and west. These are called cardinal directions. Usually these directions on a map are indicated by a compass rose.

Map Title Maps in this book have titles. The map title names the area shown on the map. A map title can include additional identification, such as population, political boundaries, or a particular period in history.

Locator Map A locator map highlights the area of the main map on a small map of Earth. Locator maps help readers understand the region they are studying.

Inset Map An inset map is a small map set onto a larger map. It may show an area that is too small or too far away to be included on the main map. The inset map on this page calls out a more detailed map of the Himalaya, Earth's highest mountains.

Scale A map scale helps you to determine the relationship between real distances on Earth and the same distances represented on the map.

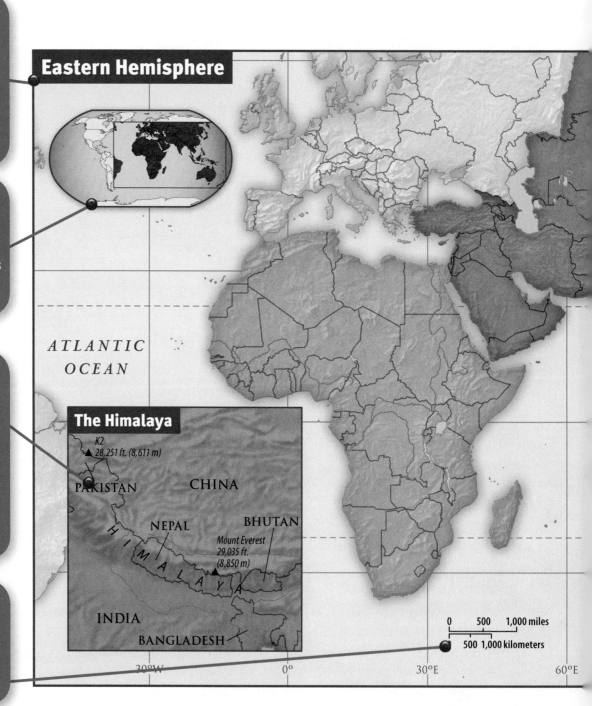

Eastern Hemisphere

The Himalaya

K2
▲ 28,251 ft. (8,611 m)

PAKISTAN   CHINA

NEPAL   BHUTAN

Mount Everest
29,035 ft.
(8,850 m)

H I M A L A Y A

INDIA

BANGLADESH

ATLANTIC
OCEAN

0   500   1,000 miles
500 1,000 kilometers

30°W   0°   30°E   60°E

The areas between cardinal directions are called intermediate directions. These are northeast, northwest, southeast, and southwest. Intermediate directions let us describe a place in relation to another place. This is called the relative location of a place. If you look on the map on this page, you can see that the relative location of Australia and Oceania is southeast of Asia.

What kind of detailed information is given in the inset map?

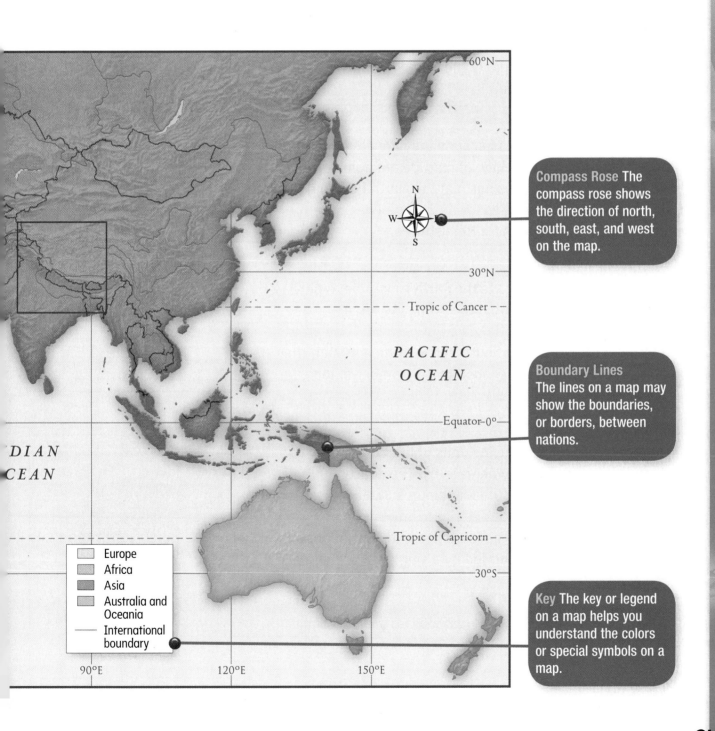

Compass Rose The compass rose shows the direction of north, south, east, and west on the map.

Boundary Lines The lines on a map may show the boundaries, or borders, between nations.

Key The key or legend on a map helps you understand the colors or special symbols on a map.

PACIFIC OCEAN

60°N

30°N

Tropic of Cancer

Equator-0°

Tropic of Capricorn

30°S

DIAN CEAN

Europe
Africa
Asia
Australia and Oceania
International boundary

90°E   120°E   150°E

Understand Earth

Hemispheres

Earth is often shown as a sphere, or a ball shape. A hemisphere is half of a sphere. Geographers have divided Earth into hemispheres. The area north of the equator is called the Northern Hemisphere. The area south of the equator is called the Southern Hemisphere.

The Prime Meridian runs north-south through Greenwich, England. Everything east of the Prime Meridian for 180 degrees is the Eastern Hemisphere. Everything west of the Prime Meridian for 180 degrees is the Western Hemisphere.

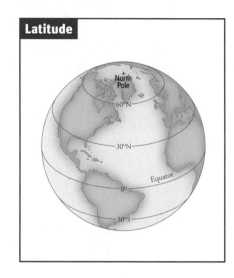

Latitude

Lines of latitude are called parallels because they are always at an equal distance from one another. Lines of latitude are numbered from 0 at the equator to 90 degrees north at the North Pole and 90 degrees south at the South Pole. Maps with latitude lines have N or S to indicate the Northern or Southern Hemisphere.

Longitude

Lines of longitude, or meridians, circle the Earth from pole to pole. These lines measure the distance from the Prime Meridian, 0 degrees longitude. Lines of longitude are not parallel. They grow closer together near the North and South Poles. At the equator, they are far apart. Maps have an E or a W next to the number to indicate the Eastern or Western Hemisphere.

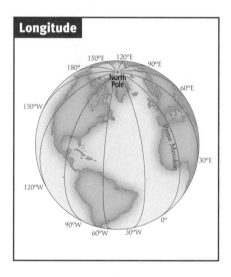

Absolute Location

You can locate any place on Earth using lines of latitude and longitude. Each line is identified by degrees (°). The spaces between the degree lines are measured in minutes ('). Each location has a unique number where one line of latitude intersects, or crosses, a line of longitude. This is absolute location. Each spot on Earth has an absolute location identified by a single set of degrees and minutes.

Think About It What is your absolute location? Use the map of the United States on page GH23 to find the lines of latitude and longitude that are closest to your home.

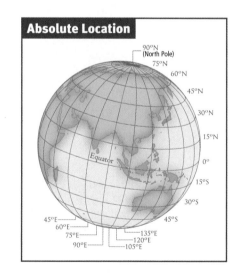

Special Purpose Maps

Some maps show specific information about a place or a period in history. These specific maps are called special purpose maps. One type of special purpose map may show how many people live in an area. Another may show the roads of a region. Still another might show the movement of an army during a historic battle.

Historical Maps

Some special purpose maps capture a period in time. These are called historical maps. They show information about past events, and the places where they occurred. Read the title of the map on this page and study the key to understand its information. The map shows information about a battle in 31 B.C. between Antony, a Roman general, and Octavian, the ruler of Rome. Octavian won the Battle of Actium. Antony's defeat helped Octavian to become the absolute ruler of the Mediterranean world.

Think About It Why might Octavian have placed his ships across the entrance to the Gulf of Ambracia?

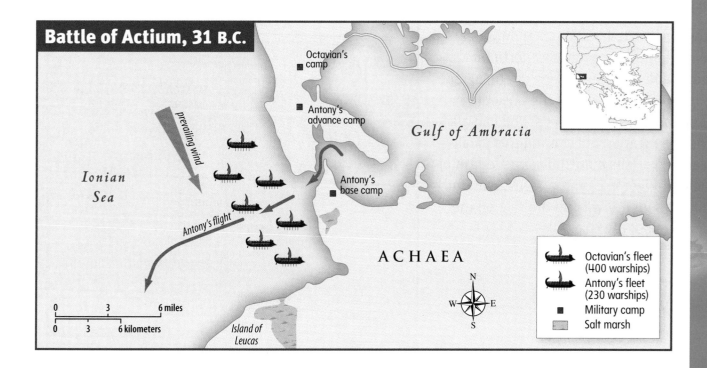

Battle of Actium, 31 B.C.

Octavian's camp

Antony's advance camp

Gulf of Ambracia

prevailing wind

Ionian Sea

Antony's base camp

Antony's flight

ACHAEA

0   3   6 miles
0   3   6 kilometers

Island of Leucas

Octavian's fleet (400 warships)
Antony's fleet (230 warships)
Military camp
Salt marsh

Maps at Different Scales

If you drew a map of the United States at its real size, your map would have to be over 3,000 miles wide. The Mississippi River on your map would be more than 2,000 miles long! A map this size would be too big to use!

So mapmakers draw maps to scale. A map scale uses some unit of measurement, such as an inch, to represent a certain number of miles or kilometers on Earth. If a map of the United States used one inch to represent a thousand miles—how wide would the United States be on the map?

Small-Scale Maps

Some maps show a large area, such as a continent, or a region. Imagine that you are in a satellite orbiting Earth. Your space ship is 100 miles above the Nile Valley. From this altitude, you can see the entire river and the surrounding river valley. Everything looks very small—like the locations on a a small-scale map. Because it covers such a large area, a small-scale map does not show many details.

From your satellite, you might notice some lights about halfway north on the Nile River. The modern city of Luxor is located on the site of the ancient Egyptian capital of Thebes. You can also find the location of Luxor on this small-scale map. This map shows the length of the Nile River in Egypt, and you can find Luxor about halfway up the Nile on the east bank of the river.

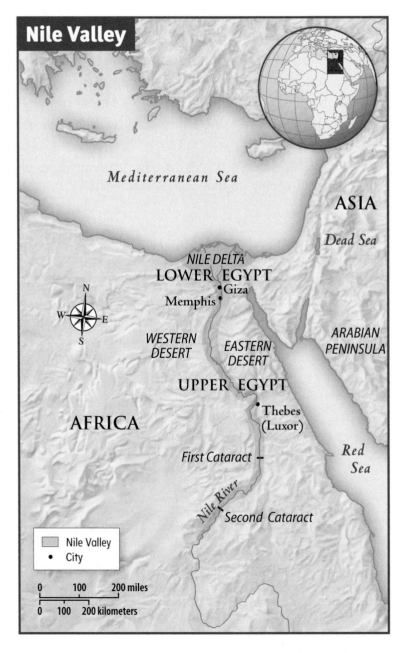

Large-Scale Maps

Now imagine that your satellite is flying only a few miles above Earth. You can see only a small area of the Nile Valley. However, you can see buildings and ancient monuments. You can also see roads and highways. This is like looking at a a large-scale map. The large-scale map shows a small area, but has more detail than a small-scale map.

The large-scale map on this page shows the streets of the modern city of Luxor. The ruins of many ancient Egyptian buildings can still be seen in Luxor. If you wanted to find the Temple of Karnak in Luxor, for example, you would use the large-scale map that shows only the city of Luxor and some of the more important buildings in the city.

Compare the scales on the two maps. What is the scale on page GH10? Is it larger or smaller than the scale on page GH11? Why do you think this is so? People choose the map that contains the information they need.

Think About It

Why might you want to have large-scale maps and small-scale maps if you are planning a trip to Egypt?

Luxor, Egypt, Today

Luxor

Open Air Museum

Karnak Temple Complex

Avenue of the Sphinxes

Nile River

Cornishe

To Airport →

Pola Hotel

Youth Hostel

Al-Karnak

Luxor Museum

Luxor

To Archaeological Sites ←

Faluccas

Tourist Ferry

Mena Palace Hotel

Station St.

Faluccas

Luxor Temple

Train Station

Tourist Ferry

Luxor Hotel

N

W E

S

Winter Palace Hotel

| 0 | .5 | 1 mile |
| 0 | .5 | 1 kilometer |

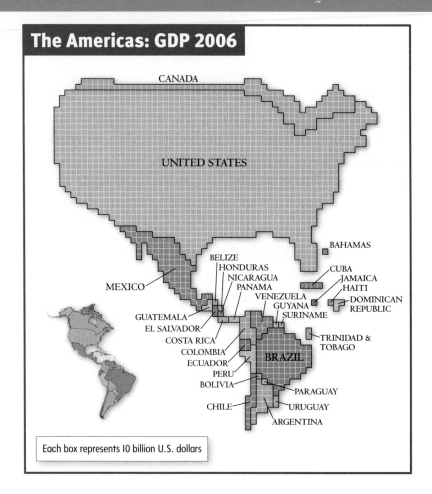

The Americas: GDP 2006

Each box represents 10 billion U.S. dollars

Use a Cartogram

A cartogram is a special kind of map that helps you to compare information about countries on the map. A cartogram does not show the physical sizes of countries. It compares information about countries, such as populations or economies. A country that is geographically quite large, such as Canada, may appear small on a cartogram comparing the size of the national economies of North America.

It is important to understand that a cartogram compares information among nations. You need to read the title of a cartogram to understand what is being compared. It may be population, or economies, or how much is spent on health and welfare by each nation in the cartogram.

You will also need to bring some of your own knowledge to read a cartogram. You have to know that Canada is one of the largest countries in the world to understand that its economy is not as large as its land size.

Think About It Why might the sizes of countries get larger or smaller on different cartograms?

Time Zone Map

You may already know that people who live in different states set their clocks at different times. This happens because the Earth spins. Where the sun is shining in one area, it is dark in another. If it were the same time all over Earth, the sun would be shining in the middle of the night at some point on our planet.

This is why Earth is divided into 24 time zones. Each time zone is set to a different hour of the day. To help you figure out what time it is someplace else in the world, you would use a Time Zone Map. This kind of map shows the number of hours that any place is ahead or behind the time at the Prime Meridian.

For example, find Moscow on the map. The time in Moscow is five hours behind the time in Irkutsk. As you traveled west, you would advance the calendar date one day. As you traveled east, you would lose one day.

Think About It Why do you think the lines on the time zone map are not perfectly straight when they go across nations?

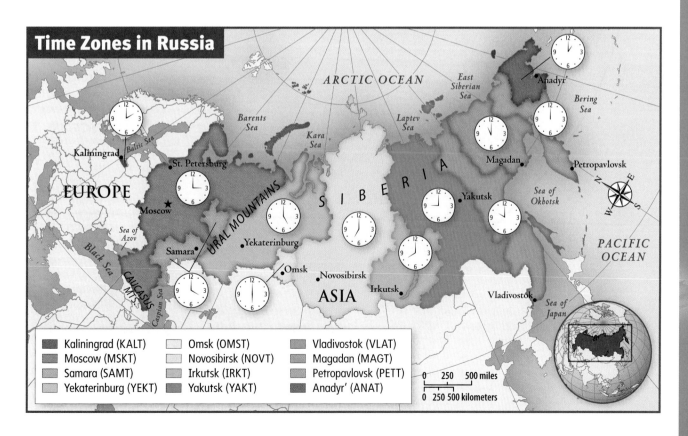

Time Zones in Russia

■ Kaliningrad (KALT)	□ Omsk (OMST)	■ Vladivostok (VLAT)	
■ Moscow (MSKT)	□ Novosibirsk (NOVT)	■ Magadan (MAGT)	
■ Samara (SAMT)	■ Irkutsk (IRKT)	■ Petropavlovsk (PETT)	
□ Yekaterinburg (YEKT)	■ Yakutsk (YAKT)	■ Anadyr' (ANAT)	

0   250   500 miles
0 250 500 kilometers

160°W   120°W   80°W   40°W

80°N

ARCTIC OCEAN

GREENLAND

Mackenzie River

60°N — ALASKA RANGE

Mt. McKinley
20,320 ft.
(6,194 m)

Arctic Circle

ROCKY MOUNTAINS

NORTH
AMERICA

CANADIAN SHIELD

40°N

Mississippi River

APPALACHIAN MTS.

PACIFIC OCEAN

ATLANTIC
OCEAN

Tropic of Cancer

20°N

Rio
Grande

Gulf of
Mexico

Caribbean Sea

0°   Equator

Amazon River

SOUTH
AMERICA

ANDES

20°S

Tropic of Capricorn

MOUNTAINS

Mt. Aconcagua
22,834 ft.
(6,960 m)

ATLANTIC
OCEAN

40°S

PACIFIC OCEAN

Cape Horn

60°S

Antarctic Circle

80°W

Weddell
Sea

120°W

40°W

160°W

Vinson Massif
16,067 ft.
(4,897 m)

ARCTIC OCEAN

40°E 80°E 120°E 160°E

80°N

Lena River

Yenisey River

Ob River

60°N

URAL MTS.

Volga River

Sea of Okhotsk

EUROPE

ALPS

Mont Blanc
15,711 ft.
(4,807 m)

Caspian Sea

Black Sea   ▲ Mt. Elbrus
              18,510 ft.
              (5,642 m)

ASIA

GOBI

40°N

HINDU KUSH

Mediterranean Sea

SYRIAN
DESERT

HIMALAYA

Yangtze River

Tropic of Cancer

S A H A R A

River

Red Sea

Ganges River

▲ Mt. Everest
29,035 ft.
(8,850 m)

20°N

DECCAN
PLATEAU

Nile

Arabian
Sea

South
China
Sea

Philippine
Sea

PACIFIC OCEAN

AFRICA

Congo River

Mt. Kilimanjaro
19,340 ft.
(5,895 m)
▲

Equator   0°

INDIAN

OCEAN

Coral
Sea

NAMIB DESERT

KALAHARI
DESERT

Tropic of Capricorn

GREAT
SANDY
DESERT

20°S

AUSTRALIA

Cape of
Good Hope

Darling River

Mt. Kosciuszko
7,310 ft.
(2,228 m)
▲

N

W   E

S

40°S

0   1,000   2,000 miles

0   1,000   2,000 kilometers

40°E 80°E 120°E 160°E

60°S

Antarctic Circle

ANTARCTICA

80°S

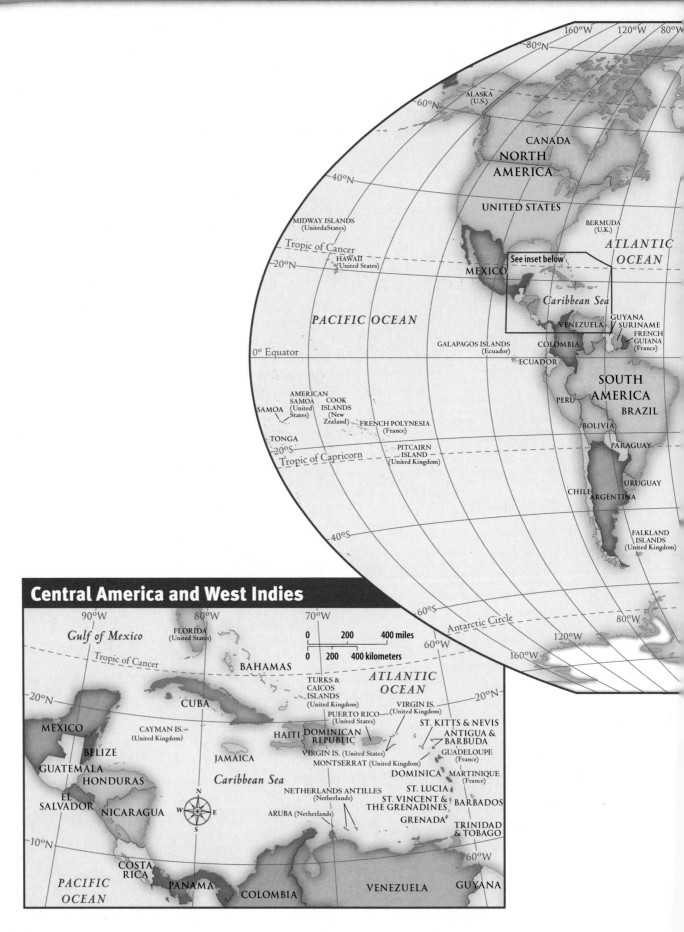

Central America and West Indies

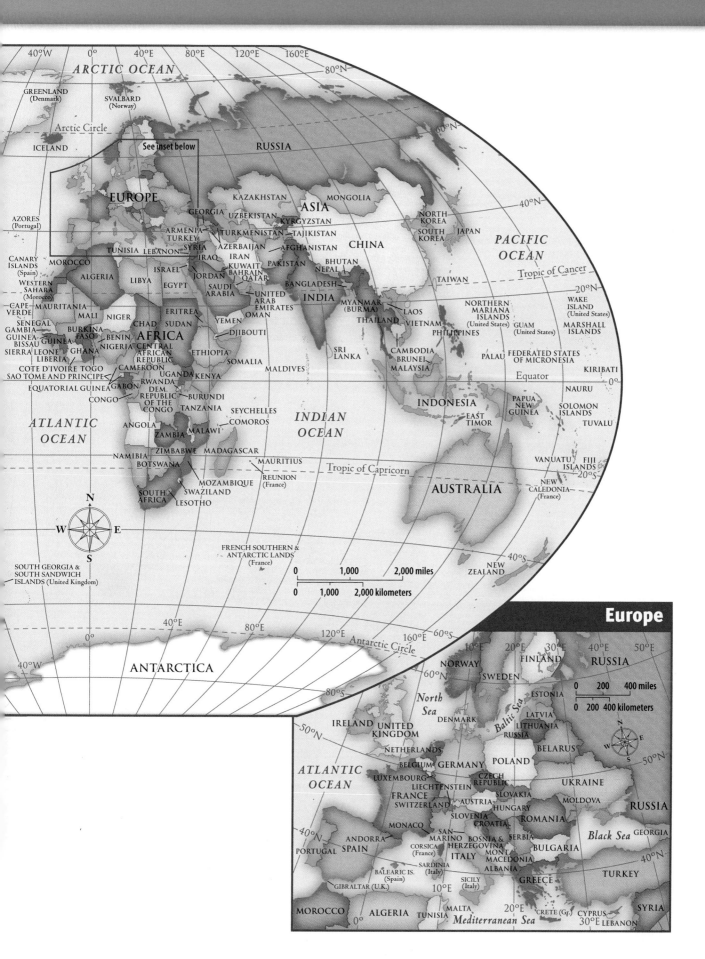

ARCTIC OCEAN

GREENLAND (Denmark)

SVALBARD (Norway)

Arctic Circle

ICELAND

See inset below

RUSSIA

EUROPE

ASIA

AZORES (Portugal)

KAZAKHSTAN

MONGOLIA

GEORGIA

UZBEKISTAN

KYRGYZSTAN

NORTH KOREA

ARMENIA

TURKMENISTAN

TAJIKISTAN

SOUTH KOREA

JAPAN

PACIFIC OCEAN

TURKEY

CANARY ISLANDS (Spain)

TUNISIA

LEBANON

SYRIA

AZERBAIJAN

AFGHANISTAN

CHINA

MOROCCO

IRAQ

IRAN

PAKISTAN

BHUTAN

NEPAL

Tropic of Cancer

ISRAEL

KUWAIT

BAHRAIN

TAIWAN

ALGERIA

LIBYA

JORDAN

QATAR

BANGLADESH

WESTERN SAHARA (Morocco)

EGYPT

SAUDI ARABIA

UNITED ARAB EMIRATES

INDIA

MYANMAR (BURMA)

LAOS

NORTHERN MARIANA ISLANDS (United States)

WAKE ISLAND (United States)

20°N

CAPE VERDE

MAURITANIA

MALI

NIGER

ERITREA

SUDAN

YEMEN

OMAN

THAILAND

VIETNAM

GUAM (United States)

MARSHALL ISLANDS

SENEGAL

CHAD

DJIBOUTI

PHILIPPINES

GAMBIA

BURKINA FASO

GUINEA BISSAU

GUINEA

BENIN

NIGERIA

AFRICA

CENTRAL AFRICAN REPUBLIC

ETHIOPIA

SRI LANKA

CAMBODIA

BRUNEI

MALAYSIA

PALAU

FEDERATED STATES OF MICRONESIA

SIERRA LEONE

GHANA

Equator

KIRIBATI

LIBERIA

COTE D'IVOIRE

TOGO

CAMEROON

UGANDA

KENYA

SOMALIA

MALDIVES

NAURU

SAO TOME AND PRINCIPE

EQUATORIAL GUINEA

GABON

RWANDA

DEM. REPUBLIC OF THE CONGO

BURUNDI

INDONESIA

PAPUA NEW GUINEA

SOLOMON ISLANDS

CONGO

TANZANIA

SEYCHELLES

INDIAN OCEAN

EAST TIMOR

TUVALU

ATLANTIC OCEAN

ANGOLA

MALAWI

COMOROS

ZAMBIA

ZIMBABWE

MADAGASCAR

NAMIBIA

BOTSWANA

MAURITIUS

Tropic of Capricorn

VANUATU

FIJI ISLANDS

20°S

REUNION (France)

AUSTRALIA

NEW CALEDONIA (France)

MOZAMBIQUE

SWAZILAND

SOUTH AFRICA

LESOTHO

N

W   E

S

SOUTH GEORGIA & SOUTH SANDWICH ISLANDS (United Kingdom)

FRENCH SOUTHERN & ANTARCTIC LANDS (France)

0   1,000   2,000 miles

0   1,000 2,000 kilometers

NEW ZEALAND

40°S

40°E

80°E

120°E

160°E

60°S

Antarctic Circle

ANTARCTICA

80°S

Europe

NORWAY

FINLAND

RUSSIA

SWEDEN

ESTONIA

North Sea

Baltic Sea

LATVIA

0   200   400 miles

0   200 400 kilometers

IRELAND

UNITED KINGDOM

DENMARK

LITHUANIA

RUSSIA

BELARUS

N

W   E

S

NETHERLANDS

BELGIUM

GERMANY

POLAND

ATLANTIC OCEAN

LUXEMBOURG

CZECH REPUBLIC

UKRAINE

LIECHTENSTEIN

FRANCE

SWITZERLAND

AUSTRIA

SLOVAKIA

HUNGARY

MOLDOVA

RUSSIA

SLOVENIA

ROMANIA

MONACO

CROATIA

ANDORRA

SAN MARINO

BOSNIA & HERZEGOVINA

SERBIA

Black Sea

GEORGIA

PORTUGAL

SPAIN

CORSICA (France)

ITALY

MONT.

MACEDONIA

BULGARIA

SARDINIA (Italy)

ALBANIA

TURKEY

BALEARIC IS. (Spain)

SICILY (Italy)

GREECE

GIBRALTAR (U.K.)

MOROCCO

ALGERIA

TUNISIA

MALTA

Mediterranean Sea

CRETE (Gr.)

CYPRUS

SYRIA

LEBANON

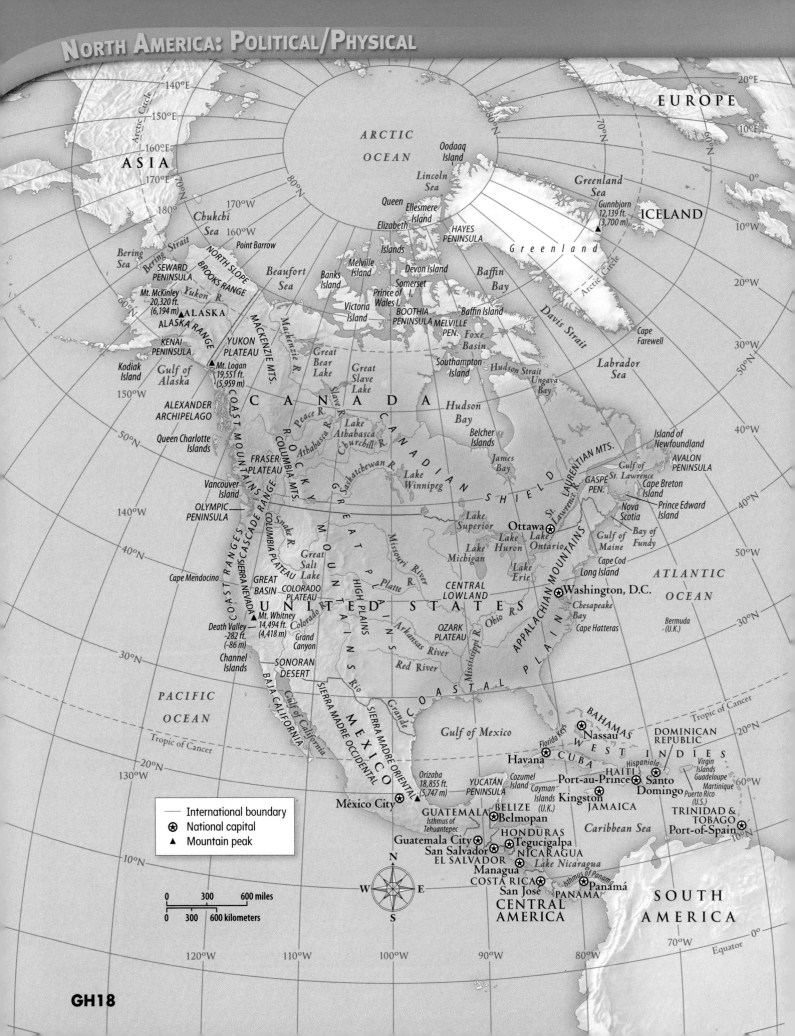

EUROPE

ASIA

ARCTIC OCEAN

Oodaaq Island

Lincoln Sea

Greenland Sea

Gunnbjorn 12,139 ft. (3,700 m) ▲

ICELAND

Chukchi Sea

Queen Elizabeth Islands

Ellesmere Island

HAYES PENINSULA

Greenland

Point Barrow

NORTH SLOPE

BROOKS RANGE

Beaufort Sea

Banks Island

Melville Island

Devon Island

Baffin Bay

Bering Sea

Bering Strait

SEWARD PENINSULA

Yukon R.

Mt. McKinley 20,320 ft. (6,194 m) ▲

ALASKA

ALASKA RANGE

KENAI PENINSULA

Victoria Island

Prince of Wales I.

Somerset Island

BOOTHIA PENINSULA

MELVILLE PEN.

Baffin Island

Foxe Basin

Davis Strait

Cape Farewell

Arctic Circle

Kodiak Island

Gulf of Alaska

YUKON PLATEAU

Mt. Logan 19,551 ft. (5,959 m) ▲

MACKENZIE MTS.

Mackenzie R.

Great Bear Lake

Great Slave Lake

C A N A D A

Hudson Strait

Ungava Bay

Labrador Sea

ALEXANDER ARCHIPELAGO

COAST MOUNTAINS

Peace R.

Slave R.

Lake Athabasca

Southampton Island

Hudson Bay

Queen Charlotte Islands

FRASER PLATEAU

ROCKY

Athabasca R.

Churchill R.

Saskatchewan R.

C A N A D I A N   S H I E L D

Belcher Islands

James Bay

Island of Newfoundland

AVALON PENINSULA

Vancouver Island

COLUMBIA MTS.

Lake Winnipeg

LAURENTIAN MTS.

GASPÉ PEN.

Gulf of St. Lawrence

Cape Breton Island

OLYMPIC PENINSULA

CASCADE RANGE

MOUNTAINS

Lake Superior

Ottawa ⊛

St. Lawrence R.

Nova Scotia

Prince Edward Island

COAST RANGES

SIERRA NEVADA

COLUMBIA PLATEAU

Snake R.

Great Salt Lake

GREAT BASIN

Missouri River

Lake Michigan

Lake Huron

Lake Ontario

Lake Erie

Gulf of Maine

Bay of Fundy

Cape Cod

Long Island

ATLANTIC OCEAN

Cape Mendocino

Great Salt Lake

COLORADO PLATEAU

GREAT PLAINS

Platte R.

CENTRAL LOWLAND

APPALACHIAN MOUNTAINS

Washington, D.C. ⊛

Chesapeake Bay

Death Valley -282 ft. (-86 m)

Mt. Whitney 14,494 ft. (4,418 m) ▲

U N I T E D   S T A T E S

Colorado R.

Grand Canyon

Arkansas River

OZARK PLATEAU

Ohio R.

Cape Hatteras

Bermuda (U.K.)

Channel Islands

SONORAN DESERT

HIGH PLAINS

Red River

Mississippi R.

COASTAL PLAIN

BAJA CALIFORNIA

Gulf of California

SIERRA MADRE OCCIDENTAL

Rio Grande

M E X I C O

SIERRA MADRE ORIENTAL

PACIFIC OCEAN

Tropic of Cancer

Gulf of Mexico

BAHAMAS

Nassau ⊛

Tropic of Cancer

DOMINICAN REPUBLIC

Florida Keys

Havana ⊛

CUBA

W E S T   I N D I E S

Hispaniola

Virgin Islands Guadeloupe

Martinique

Orizaba 18,855 ft. (5,747 m) ▲

YUCATÁN PENINSULA

Cozumel Island

Cayman Islands (U.K.)

HAITI

Port-au-Prince ⊛

⊛ Santo Domingo

Puerto Rico (U.S.)

México City ⊛

Kingston ⊛

JAMAICA

TRINIDAD & TOBAGO

GUATEMALA

Isthmus of Tehuantepec

BELIZE

Belmopan ⊛

Caribbean Sea

Port-of-Spain ⊛

Guatemala City ⊛

San Salvador ⊛

EL SALVADOR

HONDURAS

Tegucigalpa ⊛

NICARAGUA

Managua ⊛

Lake Nicaragua

COSTA RICA

San José ⊛

Isthmus of Panama

PANAMA

⊛ Panamá

SOUTH AMERICA

CENTRAL AMERICA

—— International boundary

⊛ National capital

▲ Mountain peak

0   300   600 miles

0   300   600 kilometers

N W E S

SOUTH AMERICA: POLITICAL/PHYSICAL

NORTH AMERICA

ISTHMUS OF PANAMA

Caribbean Sea

Maracaibo

Caracas

Orinoco R.

VENEZUELA

GUIANA HIGHLANDS

Georgetown

GUYANA

Paramaribo

SURINAME

Cayenne

FRENCH GUIANA (France)

Bogotá

Cali

COLOMBIA

Negro River

Quito

Equator

ECUADOR

Guayaquil

Galápagos Islands (Ecuador)

Amazon River

AMAZON BASIN

River

Tapajos River

Xingú River

Tocantins River

São Francisco River

PERU

Lima

ANDES MOUNTAINS

Madeira River

River

Lake Titicaca

La Paz

BOLIVIA

Santa Cruz

Sucre

Arequipa

BRAZIL

BRAZILIAN

Brasília

River

HIGHLANDS

ATACAMA DESERT

Mt. Ojos del Salado 22,572 ft. (6,880 m)

Paraguay R.

Paraná

PARAGUAY

Asunción

CHILE

Mt. Aconcagua 22,834 ft. (6,960 m)

ANDES MOUNTAINS

Valparaíso

Santiago

Rosario

ARGENTINA

PAMPAS

Concepción

Paraná

River

Salto

URUGUAY

Montevideo

Buenos Aires

Rio de la Plata

São Paulo

Rio de Janeiro

Tropic of Capricorn

Tropic of Capricorn

PACIFIC OCEAN

ATLANTIC OCEAN

ATLANTIC OCEAN

PATAGONIA

Falkland Islands (Islas Malvinas) (U.K.)

Strait of Magellan

TIERRA DEL FUEGO

Cape Horn

South Georgia (U.K.)

N
W E
S

15°N

15°N

Equator

0°

0°

15°S

15°S

30°S

30°S

45°S

45°S

105°W   90°W   75°W   60°W   45°W   30°W

——	International boundary
⊛	National capital
•	Other city
▲	Mountain peak

0   250   500 miles
0   250   500 kilometers

GH19

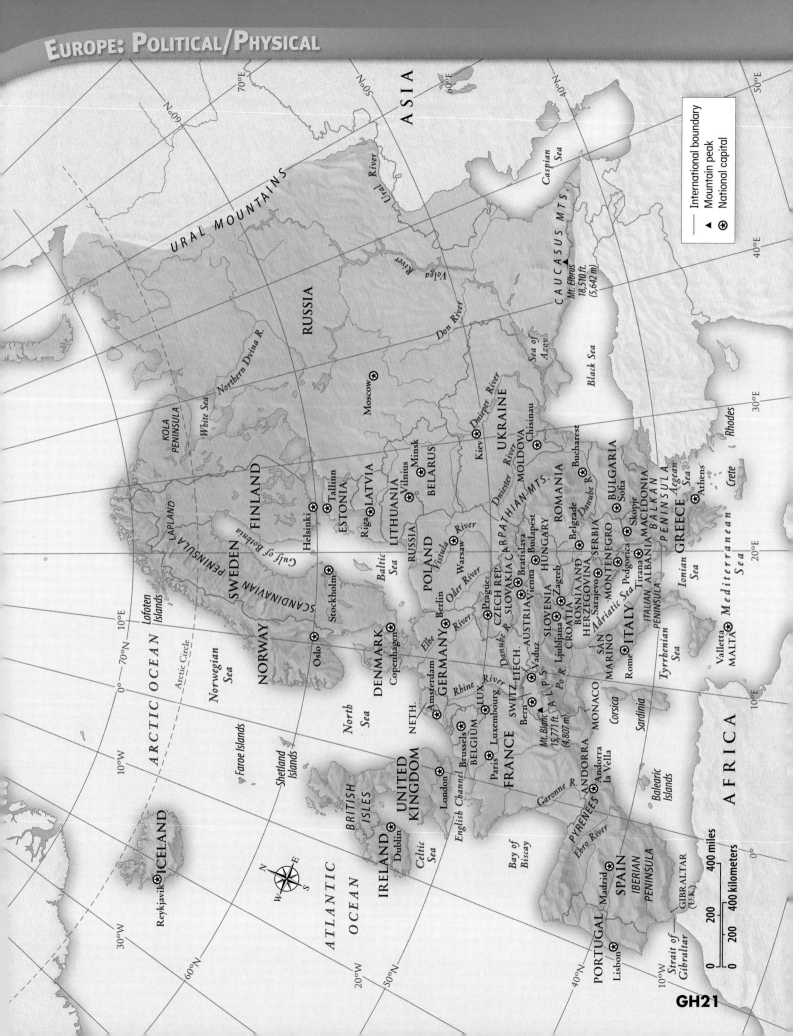

ASIA

URAL MOUNTAINS

Ural River

RUSSIA

Volga River

Caspian Sea

CAUCASUS MTS.

Mt. Elbrus
18,510 ft.
(5,642 m)

Don River

Sea of Azov

Black Sea

Northern Dwina R.

White Sea

KOLA PENINSULA

Moscow

Dnieper River

UKRAINE

Chisinau

Bucharest

ROMANIA

Danube R.

BULGARIA

Sofia

Kiev

MOLDOVA

Dniester River

CARPATHIAN MTS.

Tallinn

ESTONIA

Riga LATVIA

LITHUANIA

Vilnius

Minsk

BELARUS

RUSSIA

POLAND

Vistula

Warsaw

Oder River

SLOVAKIA

Budapest

HUNGARY

Bratislava

Belgrade

SERBIA

MONTENEGRO

Podgorica

Skopje

MACEDONIA

BALKAN PENINSULA

GREECE

Athens

Aegean Sea

Rhodes

Crete

Helsinki

FINLAND

Gulf of Bothnia

Baltic Sea

LAPLAND

SWEDEN

SCANDINAVIAN PENINSULA

Stockholm

Lofoten Islands

NORWAY

Oslo

Norwegian Sea

Arctic Circle

ARCTIC OCEAN

Faroe Islands

Shetland Islands

North Sea

DENMARK

Copenhagen

NETH.

Amsterdam

Elbe

GERMANY

Berlin

Prague

CZECH REP.

Danube R.

AUSTRIA

Vienna

Rhine

Rivers

SLOVENIA

Ljubljana

Zagreb

CROATIA

BOSNIA AND HERZEGOVINA

Sarajevo

Adriatic Sea

SAN MARINO

ITALY

Rome

Tyrrhenian Sea

Tirana

ALBANIA

ITALIAN PENINSULA

Ionian Sea

Mediterranean Sea

Valletta

MALTA

LUX.

Luxembourg

BELGIUM

Brussels

Paris

FRANCE

SWITZ. LIECH.

Bern

Vaduz

ALPS

Mt. Blanc
15,771 ft.
(4,807 m)

Po R.

MONACO

Corsica

Sardinia

Balearic Islands

AFRICA

UNITED KINGDOM

London

BRITISH ISLES

English Channel

IRELAND

Dublin

Celtic Sea

ATLANTIC OCEAN

Bay of Biscay

Garonne R.

PYRENEES

ANDORRA

Andorra la Vella

Ebro River

SPAIN

Madrid

IBERIAN PENINSULA

GIBRALTAR (U.K.)

Strait of Gibraltar

PORTUGAL

Lisbon

ICELAND

Reykjavik

Reykjavík

N E W S

0   200   400 miles

0   200   400 kilometers

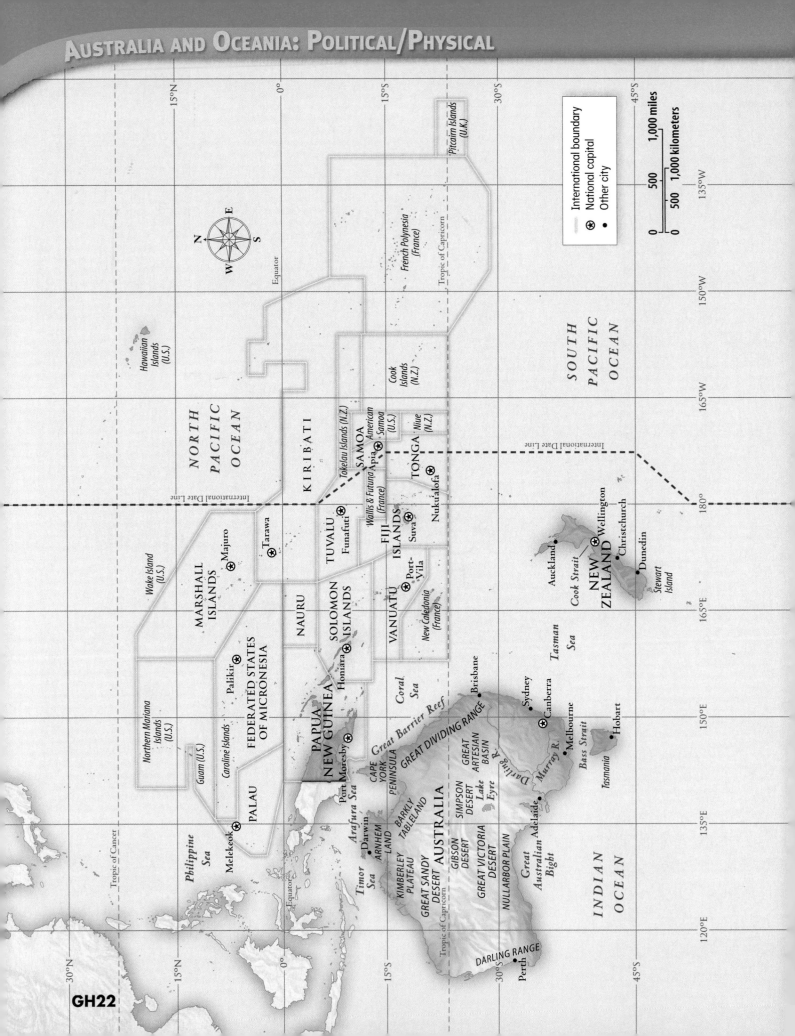

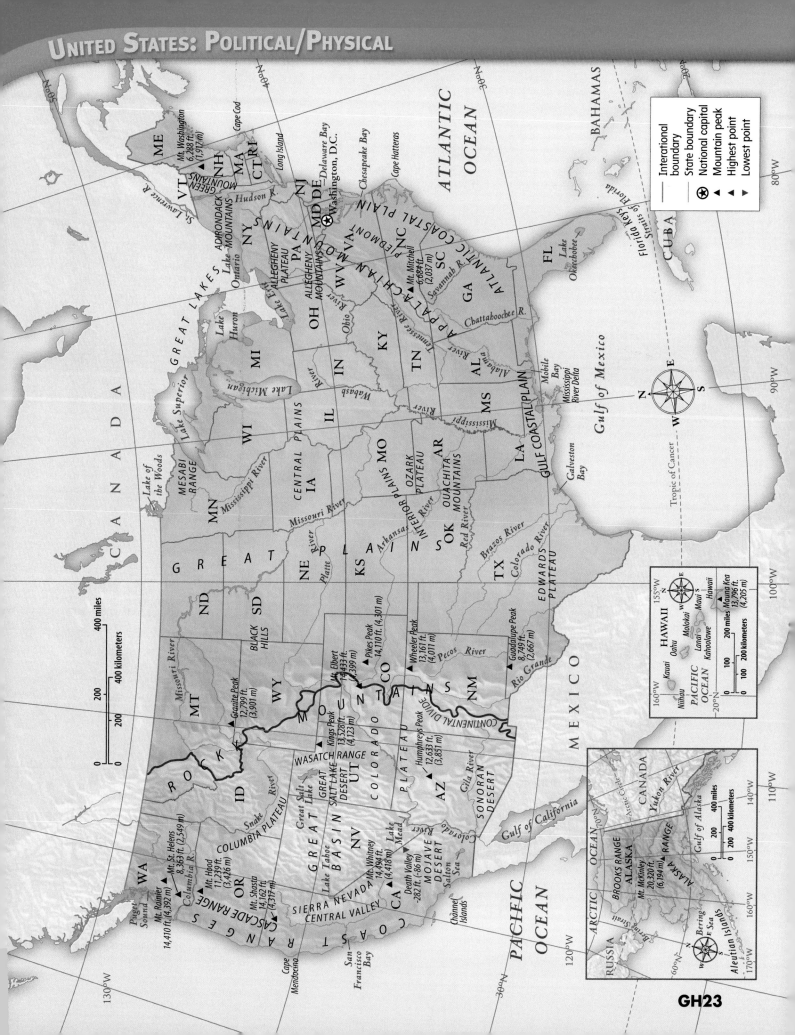

UNITED STATES: POLITICAL/PHYSICAL

Legend:
- International boundary
- State boundary
- ⊛ National capital
- ▲ Mountain peak
- ▲ Highest point
- ▶ Lowest point

Main map labels:

CANADA

ATLANTIC OCEAN

BAHAMAS

CUBA

PACIFIC OCEAN

Gulf of Mexico

MEXICO

GREAT PLAINS

GREAT LAKES

Lake Superior, Lake Huron, Lake Michigan, Lake Erie, Lake Ontario

ROCKY MOUNTAINS

APPALACHIAN MOUNTAINS

CONTINENTAL DIVIDE

States: ME, NH, VT, MA, CT, RI, NY, PA, NJ, DE, MD, WV, VA, NC, SC, GA, FL, OH, IN, KY, TN, AL, MS, LA, MI, WI, IL, MN, IA, MO, AR, ND, SD, NE, KS, OK, TX, MT, WY, CO, NM, AZ, UT, NV, ID, OR, WA, CA

Physical features and peaks:
- Mt. Washington 6,288 ft. (1,917 m)
- Cape Cod
- Long Island
- Delaware Bay
- Washington, D.C.
- Chesapeake Bay
- Cape Hatteras
- Mt. Mitchell 6,684 ft. (2,037 m)
- Lake Okeechobee
- Florida Keys
- Straits of Florida
- ADIRONDACK MOUNTAINS
- GREEN MOUNTAINS
- St. Lawrence R.
- Hudson R.
- ALLEGHENY PLATEAU
- ALLEGHENY MOUNTAINS
- PIEDMONT
- ATLANTIC COASTAL PLAIN
- Savannah R.
- Tennessee River
- Chattahoochee R.
- Ohio River
- Wabash River
- Alabama River
- Mobile Bay
- Mississippi River Delta
- GULF COASTAL PLAIN
- Galveston Bay
- Tropic of Cancer
- MESABI RANGE
- Lake of the Woods
- Mississippi River
- Missouri River
- CENTRAL PLAINS
- OZARK PLATEAU
- OUACHITA MOUNTAINS
- INTERIOR PLAINS
- Arkansas River
- Red River
- Platte River
- Brazos River
- Colorado River
- EDWARDS PLATEAU
- Pecos River
- Rio Grande
- BLACK HILLS
- Granite Peak 12,799 ft. (3,901 m)
- Mt. Elbert 14,433 ft. (4,399 m)
- Pikes Peak 14,110 ft. (4,301 m)
- Wheeler Peak 13,161 ft. (4,011 m)
- Guadalupe Peak 8,749 ft. (2,667 m)
- Kings Peak 13,528 ft. (4,123 m)
- Humphreys Peak 12,633 ft. (3,851 m)
- WASATCH RANGE
- COLORADO PLATEAU
- Gila River
- SONORAN DESERT
- Great Salt Lake
- GREAT SALT LAKE DESERT
- GREAT BASIN
- Snake River
- Columbia R.
- COLUMBIA PLATEAU
- Mt. St. Helens 8,363 ft. (2,549 m)
- Mt. Hood 11,239 ft. (3,426 m)
- Mt. Shasta 14,162 ft. (4,317 m)
- Mt. Rainier 14,410 ft. (4,392 m)
- Puget Sound
- CASCADE RANGE
- COAST RANGES
- SIERRA NEVADA
- Lake Tahoe
- Mt. Whitney 14,494 ft. (4,418 m)
- Death Valley -282 ft. (-86 m)
- MOJAVE DESERT
- Lake Mead
- Salton Sea
- Channel Islands
- CENTRAL VALLEY
- San Francisco Bay
- Cape Mendocino
- Gulf of California

Scale:
400 miles / 400 kilometers

Hawaii inset:
HAWAII
- Kauai, Niihau, Oahu, Molokai, Lanai, Maui, Kahoolawe, Hawaii
- Mauna Kea 13,796 ft. (4,205 m)
PACIFIC OCEAN
200 miles / 200 kilometers

Alaska inset:
ARCTIC OCEAN
Arctic Circle
BROOKS RANGE
ALASKA
CANADA
Yukon River
ALASKA RANGE
Mt. McKinley 20,320 ft. (6,194 m)
Gulf of Alaska
RUSSIA
Bering Strait
Bering Sea
Aleutian Islands
400 miles / 400 kilometers

GH23

EUROPE

ASIA

ATLANTIC OCEAN

Madeira Islands (Portugal)

Strait of Gibraltar

40°N

Mediterranean Sea

Algiers
Tunis
Rabat
MOROCCO

30°N

Canary Islands (Spain)

ATLAS MOUNTAINS

TUNISIA

Gulf of Gabes

Tripoli

Gulf of Sidra

Suez Canal

NILE DELTA

Cairo

SINAI PENINSULA

Tropic of Cancer

WESTERN SAHARA (Morocco)

Cape Blanc

ALGERIA

LIBYA

EGYPT

Nile R.

Red Sea

20°N

S   A   H   A   R   A

AHAGGAR MOUNTAINS

LIBYAN DESERT

Lake Nasser

NUBIAN DESERT

MAURITANIA

Nouakchott

TIBESTI MOUNTAINS

AIR RANGE

MALI

Niger

NIGER

CHAD

Khartoum

Atbara R.

ERITREA

Asmara

DJIBOUTI

Gulf of Aden

Dakar
SENEGAL
Banjul
GAMBIA

Senegal R.

Bamako

BURKINA FASO

Niamey

River

Lake Chad

SUDAN

White Nile R.

Blue Nile R.

Djibouti

SOMALI PENINSULA

10°N

Bissau
GUINEA-BISSAU
GUINEA

Ouagadougou

N'Djamena

ETHIOPIAN HIGHLANDS

Addis Ababa

Conakry
SIERRA LEONE
Freetown

COTE D'IVOIRE

GHANA

BENIN

NIGERIA

Abuja

CENTRAL AFRICAN REPUBLIC

SUDD

Lake Turkana

GREAT RIFT VALLEY

ETHIOPIA

SOMALIA

Monrovia
LIBERIA
Yamoussoukro
Accra
Lake Volta
TOGO
Porto-Novo
Lome

Benue River

Mogadishu

Cape Palmas

Gulf of Guinea

CAMEROON

Bangui

Lake Albert

UGANDA

Kampala

0°

Equator

EQUATORIAL GUINEA

SAO TOME AND PRINCIPE

Malabo

Yaounde

Ubangi R.

Congo R.

Lake Victoria

KENYA

Nairobi

INDIAN OCEAN

Sao Tome

Cape Lopez

Libreville

GABON

CONGO

CONGO BASIN

Lomami R.

Kigali
RWANDA
Bujumbura
BURUNDI

Lake Victoria

Mt. Kilimanjaro
19,340 ft. (5,895 m)

Pemba Island

Brazzaville

Kasai R.

Kinshasa

DEMOCRATIC REPUBLIC OF THE CONGO

Dodoma

Zanzibar Island

Dar es Salaam

SEYCHELLES

CABINDA (Angola)

Kwango R.

Luanda

Lake Tanganyika

TANZANIA

Cape Delgado

10°S

BIE PLATEAU

MALAWI

Lake Malawi

COMOROS

Moroni

Mayotte (France)

ATLANTIC OCEAN

ANGOLA

Cubango R.

Cuando R.

ZAMBIA

Lilongwe

Lusaka

Lake Kariba

Zambezi R.

Mozambique Channel

MADAGASCAR

N
W   E
S

NAMIBIA

OKAVANGO BASIN

Victoria Falls

Harare

ZIMBABWE

Limpopo R.

MOZAMBIQUE

Antananarivo

20°S

Tropic of Capricorn

Windhoek

NAMIB DESERT

KALAHARI DESERT

BOTSWANA

Gaborone

Pretoria

Maputo

SWAZILAND

Mbabane

Vaal R.

Maseru

LESOTHO

30°S

Bloemfontein

Orange River

DRAKENSBERG

Cape Town

SOUTH AFRICA

Cape of Good Hope

Cape Agulhas

40°S

⊛ National capital

—— International boundary

- - - Disputed boundary

▲ Mountain peak

≋ Waterfall

0   500   1,000 miles

0   500   1,000 kilometers

20°W   10°W   0°   10°E   20°E   30°E   40°E   50°E

Glossary

This glossary will help you to pronounce and understand the meanings of the vocabulary terms in this book. The page number at the end of the definition tells you where the word first appears.

PRONUNCIATION KEY

a	at	ē	me	ō	old	ū	use	ng	song
ā	ape	i	it	ô	fork	ü	rule	th	thin
ä	far	ī	ice	oi	oil	ù	pull	th	this
âr	care	î	pierce	ou	out	ûr	turn	zh	measure
e	end	o	hot	u	up	hw	white	ə	about, taken, pencil, lemon, circus

A

abacus (ab′ə kəs) a frame with sliding beads, used for mathematical solutions (p. 202)

adobe (ə dō′bē) clay and straw formed into sun-dried bricks (p. 113)

agriculture (ag′ri kul chər) the ways of growing crops and raising animals (p. 25)

alliance (ə lī′əns) an agreement to work together (p. 277)

ancestor (an′ses tər) a family member who lived a long time ago (p. 7)

annul (ə nəl′) to legally undo (p. 199)

anthropologist (an thrə pol′ə jist) a scientist who studies human culture (p. 7)

anti-Semitism (an tē sem′i tizm) the hatred of Jews (p. 311)

apartheid (ə pär′tīd) a legal structure supporting racial segregation in South Africa (p. 315)

aqueduct (ak′wə dukt) a bridge-like structure that carries water to cities (p. 104)

archaeologist (är kē ol′ə jist) a scientist who studies the remains of human culture (p. 7)

archipelago (är kə pel′ə gō) a cluster of many islands (p. 321)

armistice (är′mə stis) an agreement to stop fighting (p. 279)

arms race (ärmz rās) the competition to design and build the most powerful weapons (p. 304)

artifact (är′ti fakt) anything made and used by people in the past (p. 22)

artisan (är′tə zən) a skilled worker (p. 57)

astrolabe (as′trə lāb) an instrument used for navigating by the stars (p. 146)

astronomy (as tron′ə mē) the study of stars and planets (p. 38)

B

bar graph (bär graf) a graph that shows information using rectangles at different lengths (p. 153)

barter (bär′tər) to trade goods and services in payment, rather than to pay with cash or coins (p. 25)

Bastille (ba stēl′) a royal prison in Paris, France, which was attacked on July 14, 1789, beginning the French Revolution (p. 251)

bazaar (bə zär′) a market place with rows of shops and tents (p. 144)

boycott (boi′kot) a form of organized protest in which people refuse to do business with a company or nation (p. 250)

C

caliph (ka′lif) a Muslim political and religious leader in the years following the death of Muhammad (p. 141)

caravan (kar′a van) a group of traveling traders (p. 135)

caravel (kar′a vel) a cargo ship designed for ocean travel in the 1400s (p. 235)

caste (kast) a social group in Hinduism into which a person is born (p. 56)

cathedral (ka thē′drəl) a large Christian church led by a bishop (p. 187)

causeway (kôz′wā) raised roadway used for travel across water (p. 120)

census (sen′səs) a count of every person living in a country (p. 104)

century (sen′chə rē) one hundred years (p. 23)

circa (sûr′kə) around or about a certain date (p. 23)

circumnavigate (sûr kum nav′ə gāt) to sail completely around Earth (p. 237)

city-state (si′ tē stāt) a city and its nearby land and villages (p. 32)

civil disobedience (siv′əl dis ō bē′dē əns) to peacefully protest by refusing to obey laws that are felt to be unjust (p. 307)

civil service (siv′əl sûr′vis) the structure which employs people to work for a government (p. 74)

civil war (siv′əl wär) a war between groups within a country (p. 100)

climate (klī′mit) a place's weather over a long period of time (p. 2)

climograph (klī′mō graf) a graph that gives information about the weather of a place over a period of time (p. 233)

code (kōd) a collection of laws (p. 35)

codex (kō′ deks) a long book written by the Maya (p. 117)

Cold War (kōld wär) the global struggle for power between the United States and the Soviet Union (p. 303)

command economy (kə mand i kon′ ə mē) an economy completely controlled and directed by a government (p. 283)

commune (kom′ ūn) a community where labor, resources, and property are shared (p. 296)

communism (kom′ ūn izm) a political system in which government controls all land and industry (p. 281)

complex (kom′ pleks) a cluster of buildings (p. 219)

concentration camps (kon sen trā′shun kamps) prisons where Nazis enslaved and murdered millions of people (p. 286)

confederation (kon fed ə rā′ shun) an alliance of states or provinces, such as the Confederation of Canada (p. 256)

conquistador (kon kēs′ tə dôr) a Spanish conqueror of Native Americans (p. 242)

consul (kon′ səl) an elected leader of ancient Rome (p. 98)

consumer (kon sü′ mər) one who buys goods and uses services (p. 10)

contour (kon′ tür) imaginary lines that enclose areas of equal elevation on a topgraphic map (p. 45)

convent (kon′ vent) a building housing a community of nuns (p. 187)

coup (kü) a sudden overthrow of the government(p. 321)

covenant (kuv′ə nənt) an agreement or promise (p. 36)

Crusade (krü′sād) war for control of the holy land (p. 188)

cultural region (kul′chûr əl rē′jən) an area in which a culture is expressed (p. 6)

Cultural Revolution (kul′chûr əl rev ō lü′shun) the destruction of China's cultural past during the rule of Mao Zedong (p. 297)

D

daimyo (dīm′yō) a military and political leader in feudal Japan (p. 212)

decade (dek′ād) a ten-year time span (p. 23)

deity (dē′i tē) a god or a goddess (p. 56)

demand (də mand′) the desire or need for goods or services (p. 162) see **supply**

democracy (də mok′rə sə) a form of government in which citizens participate and hold ultimate power (p. 91)

depression (di presh′ ən) an era of high unemployment and economic hardship (p. 285)

dhow (dou) an Arabian boat with a large triangular sail (p. 171)

diffusion (di fü′shun) the spreading of one thing into another (p. 9)

divan (di von′) a council of advisors in the Ottoman Empire (p. 150)

divine right (di vīn′ rīt) the belief that monarchs receive the right to rule from God and that they need answer only to God (p. 249)

domesticate (də mest′ik āt) to adapt and raise wild plants and animals for agricultural needs (p. 26)

double bar graph (dub′əl bär graf) a graph that compares information with parallel rectangles (p. 101)

dynasty (dī′nə stē) a family that rules for several generations (p. 42)

E

elevation (el ə vā′shun) the height of land above sea level (p. 45)

empire (em′pīr) several territories and nations ruled by one authority (p. 32)

Enlightenment (en līt′ən ment) an era of scientific and ethical progress in Europe during the 1600s and 1700s (p. 232)

environment (en vīr′ən ment) the surroundings in which people, plants, and animals live (p. 21)

epic (ep′ik) a long poem that tells about the life of a hero (p. 62)

export (eks pôrt) a trade good which is sent to another country (p. 62) see **import**

F

factory (fak′tə rē) a building where goods are manufactured (p. 259)

fascist (fash′ist) someone who supports a political movement that combines nationalism and racism and demands total government control (p. 285)

feudalism (fü′dəl izm) political and economic system based on loyalty to a lord (p. 182)

flow chart (flō chärt) a chart that uses pictures or words to show, step by step, how something is done (p. 205)

Forbidden City (fôr bid'ən si tē) the walled complex of palaces and temples where the Chinese emperor and his court lived (p. 203)

G

genocide (jen ō sīd) the planned destruction of an ethnic, political, or cultural group (p. 289)

geocentric (jē ō sen' trik) the idea that Earth is the center of the universe (p. 229) see **heliocentric**

geography (jē og'rə fē) the study of Earth's surface (p. 2)

global economy (glō'bəl i kon'ə mē) the flow of goods, services, and currency among nations (p. 327)

globalization (glō'bəl i zā'shun) the policy of connecting nations through trade, politics, culture, and technology (p. 327)

glyph (glif) a picture symbol (p. 117)

GMT abbreviation for Greenwich Mean Time, the line of longitude where each day begins. (page 239) see **Greenwich Mean Time**

granary (grā nə rē) where grains are stored (p. 169)

Grand Mufti (grand məf'tē) the highest religious official of Sunni Islam (p. 150)

Grand Vizier (grand vi zēr') an advisor to the Ottoman sultan (p. 150)

Great Leap Forward (grāt lēp fôr'wärd) Chairman Mao's failed attempt to modernize China's economy in the 1950s (p. 296)

Green Revolution (grēn re və lü'shun) a movement to increase agricultural production in India and other countries in the 1960s (p. 308)

Greenwich Mean Time or GMT (gren' ich mēn tīm) the starting point for counting hours across the world's time zones, located in Greenwich, England (p. 239)

griot (grē'ō) a west African storyteller and keeper of oral histories (p. 164) see **oral history**

gross domestic product (grōs' də mes'tik prod' əkt) the value of all the goods and services in one nation (p. 11)

guerrilla (gə ril'ə) an armed person who uses sabotage and surprise attacks against a government or an invading military force (p. 322)

guild (gild) an organized group of artisans in the same industry or trade during the Middle Ages in Europe (p. 183)

H

harbor (här'bər) a sheltered place along a coast (p. 85)

heliocentric (hē lē ō sen' trik) a sun-centered description of the universe (p. 229) see **geocentric**

hieroglyphics (hī'ər ə glif'iks) an ancient Egyptian writing system that used picture symbols (p. 44)

historical map (his tôr'i kəl map) a map that shows places and events of the past (p. 95)

humanism (hū' mən izm) a philosophy based in human values and achievement (p. 193)

hunter-gatherer (hun'tər gath' ər ər) one who hunted animals and gathered wild plants for food (p. 21)

hydroponics (hī drō pon' iks) method of growing crops in water used widely in the Inca Empire (p. 124)

I

immunity (i mūn′i tē) resistance to a disease (p. 243)

imperialism (im pîr′ē əl izm) claiming colonies to increase a nation's wealth and power (p. 263)

import (im pôrt) a trade good that is brought into one country from another country (p. 62) see **export**

Industrial Revolution (in dəs′trē əl rev ō lü′shun) a period starting in the 1700s when goods began to be made by machines (p. 259)

inflation (in flā′ shun) period when prices shoot upward (p. 105)

infusion (in fū shun) the introduction of one substance, idea, or influence into another (p. 9)

innovation (in ō vā′shun) a new idea, or way of doing something (p. 9)

Inquisition (in kwə zi′shun) a church-run court (p. 197)

irrigation (îr ə gā shun) a system of transporting water from a river, lake, or well to make farming possible in dry region (p. 30)

J

Janissaries (jan ə sâ rē) elite Turkish soldiers of the Ottoman Empire (p. 150)

L

line graph (līn graf) a diagram that presents patterns and amounts of change over a period of time (p. 153)

loess (les) a rich yellow soil of the Huang He valley in China (p. 65)

M

manor (man′ər) an area of land controlled by a lord during the Middle Ages in Europe (p. 182)

manufacturing economy (man yə fak chər ing i kon ə mē) an economy based on production of goods (p. 12)

martial law (mär′shəl lô) temporary military rule over a population (p. 323)

mestizo (mes tē zō) a person of mixed Spanish and Native American ancestry (p. 254)

Middle Passage (mid′əl pas′ij) the distance captured Africans were shipped across the Atlantic Ocean to the West Indies (p. 246)

minaret (min ə ret′) a tower from which Muslims are called to pray (p. 145)

mint (mint) to make coins or other currency (p. 161)

Mogul (mü gəl) a Persian, Mongolian, or Turkish Muslim who lived in India (p. 207)

monarchy (mon′ər kē) a government led or directed by a king or queen (p. 91)

monastery (mon′ə ste rē) a building housing a group of monks (p. 187)

monotheism (mon ə thē′ iz əm) belief in one God (p. 36)

monsoon (mon sün′) strong wind over the Arabian Sea that changes direction, causing a wet season and a dry season over India (p. 53)

mosque (mosk) a Muslim place of worship (p. 145)

mummy (mu′mē′) a dead body that has been prepared for preservation, especially in Egypt (p. 49)

Muslim (muz′lim) one who follows Islam (p. 136)

N

nationalism (nash′ə nə liz əm) loyalty to one's country (p. 263)

NATO (nā′ tō) a military alliance formed in 1949 between nations in North America and Europe to oppose communism (p. 302)

Northwest Passage (nôrth west pas′ ij) a water route believed by explorers of the 1500s and 1600s to cross North America between the Atlantic and Pacific Oceans (p. 238)

O

oasis (ō ā′sis) a place in a desert where water can be found (p. 133)

Old Stone Age (ōld stōn āj) the earliest period of human existence before humans learned to make objects out of any metal (p. 21)

oligarchy (o′li gär kē) government based on the rule of the wealthy and powerful (p. 91)

oracle (ôr′ ə kəl) a priest believed to be able to predict the future (p. 67)

oral history (ôr′əl his′ tə rē) stories told aloud and passed from one generation to the next (p. 7)

P

papyrus (pə pī′rəs) an Egyptian reed that was used to make a kind of paper (p. 44)

parallel time line (par′ə lel tīm′līn) a diagram of events arranged in time order for two different regions or people's lives (p. 23)

patrician (pə tri′ shən) member of Rome's powerful families (p. 98)

Pax Romana (pox rō ma′ nə) a period of peace under the Roman Empire between 27 B.C. and A.D. 180 (p. 103)

pharaoh (fâr′ ō) all-powerful king in ancient Egypt (p. 42)

philosopher (fə los′ə fər) someone who seeks truth and the right way to live (p. 89)

physical region (fiz′i kəl rē′jən) a land region that shares a natural environment (p. 2)

pictograph (pik′tə graf) a graph that uses a picture that stands for an object or idea (p. 67)

picture graph (pik chər graf) a graph in which pictures or symbols represent a certain amount of something (p. 291)

pilgrimage (pil′ grə mij) a journey to a holy place or shrine (p. 137)

plague (plāg) a disease or event that causes suffering for many people (p. 93)

plebeian (pli bē′ ən) poor farmer or shopkeeper of ancient Rome (p. 98)

polytheism (pol ē thē′iz əm) belief in many gods (p. 32)

porcelain (pôr′sə lin) a special clay that can be shaped and baked to make dishes and vases (p. 202)

producer (prə dü′ sər) those who provide services or make goods (p. 10)

projection (prə jek′shən) the method of transferring the information from a globe onto a flat surface (p. 221)

propaganda (prop ə gand′ ə) spreading ideas to influence opinion (p. 285)

pueblo (pweb′lō) a Spanish name for a Southwest culture (p. 112)

pyramid (pîr′ə mid) a massive stone building with a square base and four triangular sides, used as a tomb in ancient Egypt (p. 50)

Q

quipu (kē′ pü) colored and knotted strings used by the Inca to send messages (p. 125).

R

raja (rä jə) a prince or other ruler of India (p. 59)

Reformation (re'fər mā' shən) a movement that established the Christian Protestant churches in Europe (p. 198)

refugee (ref 'yū jē') someone who flees from home to avoid death or suffering (p. 316)

reincarnation (rē in cär nā'shən) the cycle of rebirth (p. 56)

Renaissance (ren'ə säns) a period of cultural growth in Europe in the 1500s (p. 193)

republic (ri pub'lik) a government in which the leader is voted into office (p. 98)

resource distribution map (rē'sôrs dis tri bū'shən map) a map that shows where natural resources are located in a nation or region (p. 169)

S

samurai (sam'ü rī) an elite warrior of feudal Japan (p. 212)

sanction (sangk'shən) an economic, legal, or military penalty applied against one nation by another nation or group of nations (p. 315)

scribe (skrīb) a person whose job was to write or copy documents, records, and other documents in ancient times (p. 33)

serf (sûrf) a servant who farmed the land (p. 182)

service economy (sûr'vis i kon'ə mē) an economy based on providing services (p. 12)

shah (sha) the title of a Persian or Iranian monarch (p. 208)

sharia (sha rē'ə) Islamic laws that govern personal and public life (p. 312)

Shinto (shin'tō) the nature-based religion of Japan (p. 211)

shogun (shō' gən) the head of an army or military government (p. 211)

shogunate (shō' gən ət) the period when shoguns ruled Japan between ca. 800 and 1867 (p. 212)

sickle (si'kəl) a tool with a curved blade that is used to cut grain and tall grass (p. 158)

Silk Road (silk rōd) a network of trade routes across Asia stretching from China to the Mediterranean Sea (p. 75)

space race (spās rās) the challenge among world governments to explore outer space and reach the moon (p. 304)

specialize (spesh'ə līz) train to do one particular kind of work (p. 25)

sphere of influence (sfirs ov in' flū əns) an area of China that Europeans took from the Chinese government and ruled by European laws (p. 266)

standardization (stan dər dəz ā' shən) the process of making things similar (p. 71)

strait (strāt) a narrow waterway that connects larger bodies of water (p. 217)

strike (strīk) to protest working conditions by refusing to work in the factory until workers' demands are met (p. 261)

sultan (sul' tən) the monarch of a Muslim country, especially the Ottoman Empire (p. 149)

supply (sə plī') the amount of goods or services available at any time (p. 162) see **demand**

surplus (sûr' pləs) an extra amount of food, money, or other goods beyond what is needed for personal use (p. 25)

T

technology (tek nol'ə jē) tools and methods used to help humans perform tasks (p. 21)

terrace (ter'is) flat area dug out of hillsides (p. 122)

terrorist (ter′ ər ist) one who uses fear and violence to achieve political goals (p. 312)

textile (teks′tīl) cloth made from woven threads (p. 159)

theory (thē′ə rē) an explanation about how or why something happens (p. 229)

time line (tīm līn) a diagram of events arranged in the order in which they took place (p. 23)

time zone (tīm zōn) any of 24 divisions of the Earth's surface that standardizes the local time (p. 239)

topographic map (top ə graf′ik) a physical map that shows features of Earth's surface (p. 45)

totalitarian (tō tal i târ′ ē ə niz əm) government or dictator that has almost total control over people's lives (p. 283)

totem (tō′təm) an animal symbol of a group or family (p. 113)

Triangular Trade (trī ang′gyə lər trād) the trade route between Africa, the West Indies, and North America (p. 246)

tsunami (tsü nä′mē) a tidal wave caused by an undersea earthquake (p. 86)

tyrant (tī′rənt) one who rules harshly and with absolute power (p. 91)

U

union (ūn′yən) a group of workers who unite to improve working conditions (p. 261)

V

vaccine (vak sēn′) a method of preventing diseases, such as smallpox (p. 232)

values (val′ūz) principles or standards of what people consider to be important in life (p. 8)

vassal (vas′əl) one who swore loyalty to a lord (p. 182)

W

warlord (wôr lôrd) a military leader with his own army (p. 66)

Warsaw Pact (wôr sô pakt) an alliance between the Soviet Union and Eastern European communist countries organized to oppose NATO (p. 302)

Wat (wot) a Buddhist temple and school (p. 219)

Index

This index lists many topics that appear in the book, along with the pages on which they are found. Page numbers after a *c* refer you to a chart or diagram, after a *g*, to a graph, after an *m*, to a map, after a *p*, to a photograph or picture, and after a *q*, to a quotation.

Index

Index

Credits

& Co. KG/Alamy Images. 292-293: Getty Images. 293: (b) Getty Images. 294: (b) Bettmann/CORBIS. 295: William Sewell/Art Archive. 296: SV-Bilderdienst/The Image Works, Inc. 297: (b) 2005 Roger-Viollet/The Image Works, Inc.; (c) Macduff Everton/CORBIS. 298: (b) vario images GmbH & Co.KG/Alamy Images; (c) William Sewell/Art Archive. 300: (bc) AP Photos; (bl) Public Record Office/Topham-HIP/The Image Works, Inc.; (br) Getty Images. 300-301: Public Record Office/Topham-HIP/The Image Works, Inc. 302: (b) AP Photos; (t) CORBIS. 303: Gert Schütz/akg-images. 304: (b) Department of Defense; (tc) Getty Images; (tr) AP Photos. 305: (c) AP Photos; (t) Time Life Pictures/Getty Images. 306: (bl) Dagli Orti (A)/Art Archive; (br) Tom Bible/Alamy Images. 306-307: Dagli Orti (A)/Art Archive. 307: (b) Getty Images. 309: (c) Dagli Orti (A)/Art Archive; (inset) Tom Bible/Alamy Images; (t) Dinodia Photo Library. 310: (bl) Patrick Robert/Sygma/CORBIS; (br) Marco Di Lauro/Getty Images. 310-311: David Hume Kennerly/Getty Images. 311: (b) Patrick Robert/Sygma/CORBIS. 313: (b) Marco Di Lauro/Getty Images; (t) David Hume Kennerly/Getty Images. 314: (bc) EPA/CORBIS;
(bl) Paul Almasy/CORBIS; (br) Issouf Sanogo/AFP/Getty Images. 314-315: Paul Almasy/CORBIS. 315: (b) Collart Herve/CORBIS Sygma. 316: EPA/CORBIS. 318: (b) Issouf Sanogo/AFP/Getty Images; (c) Bettmann/CORBIS. 319: (b) Paul Almasy/CORBIS; (t) Mandel Ngan/AFP/Getty Images. 320: (bc) Tibor Bognar/Alamy Images; (bl) Dita Alangkara/AP Photos; (br) Morton Beebe/CORBIS. 320-321: Dita Alangkara/AP Photos. 321: (b) Choo Youn-Kong/AFP/Getty Images. 322: Tibor Bognar/CORBIS. 323: (b) Steven Mc Curry/Magnum Photos; (t) Bettmann/CORBIS. 324: (b) Morton Beebe/CORBIS. 324-325: (bkgd) Frank Chmura/Panoramic Images. 325: (c) Dita Alangkara/AP Photos; (t) Charles Lenars/CORBIS. 326: (bcl) Yann Arthus-Bertrand/CORBIS; (bcr) Jean-Marc Giboux/Getty Images; (bl) David Frazier/Getty Images; (br) Paula Bronstein/Getty Images. 326-327: CP, Fred Chartrand/AP Photos. 327: (b) Lee Foster/Bruce Coleman Inc. 328: (b) Paul A. Souders/CORBIS; (inset) Yann Arthus-Bertrand/CORBIS. 329: (b) Paul A. Souders/CORBIS; (t) James Nachtwey/VI/AP Photos. 330: (tl) Grant Neuenburg/Reuters/CORBIS; (tr) Center for Disease Control. 331: Jean-Marc Giboux/Getty Images. 332: Spencer Platt/Getty Images. 333: (b) Jean-Marc Giboux/Getty Images; (c) Paula Bronstein/Getty Images; (tl) Paula Bronstein/Getty Images; (tr) Bob Daemmrich/The Image Works, Inc. 334: (c) Time Life Pictures/Getty Images. 336: (cr) Issouf Sanogo/AFP/Getty Images; (t) Amos Morgan/Getty Images. R3: Larry Dale Gordon/Getty Images. R5: Peter Connolly/akg-images. R7: With respect to 1989.281.98 Egyptian, Ram's Head Amulet, ca. 770-657 B.C.E; Dynasty 25; late Dynastic period, gold; 1 5/8 x 1 3/8 in. (4.2 x 3.6 cm): The Metropolitan Museum of Art, Gift of Norbert Schimmel Trust, 1989 . (1989.281.98) Photograph © 1992 The Metropolitan Museum of Art. R9: Private Collection/Bridgeman Art Library. R11: Giraudon/Bridgeman Art Library. R13: Franklin D. Roosevelt Library. GH2-GH3: (t) Daryl Benson/Masterfile. GH4: (b) John Warden/Getty Images; (c) CORBIS. GH5: (b) Getty Images; (c) Ken Gillham/Robert Harding Picture Library; (t) Frans Lemmens/Getty Images.

ACKNOWLEDGMENTS

Grateful acknowledgment is given to the following authors and publishers. Every effort has been made to trace the ownership of all copyrighted material and to secure the necessary permissions to reprint these selections. In the case of some selections for which acknowledgment is not given, extensive research has failed to locate the copyright holders.